tHE DECEIVERS

THE DECEIVERS

JOSH MCDOWELL
BOB HOSTETLER
DAVID H. BELLIS

GREEN KEY BOOKS

Holiday, Florida

Library of Congress Cataloging-in-Publication Data

McDowell, Josh.
 The deceivers / Josh McDowell, Bob Hostetler, Dave Bellis.
    p. cm.
Summary: Three high school students on a wilderness trip with their church group struggle with moral decisions, while several of Satan's underlings try to lead them astray. Includes sections that relate the story to real-life decisions and matters of spiritual growth.
 ISBN 1-60-098013-9
[1. Christian life-Fiction. 2. Conduct of life-Fiction. 3. Wilderness survival-Fiction.] I. Hostetler, Bob. 2003 II. Bellis, Dave. III. Title.
 PZ7.M478446 De 2003
[Fic]-dc21

Published by Green Key Books
2514 Aloha Place
Holiday, FL 34691

Printed in the United States of America

06 07 08 09   5   4   3   2

table of contents

●●●●●●●●●●

THIS BOOK is dedicated to a very, very special granddaughter and her family, who inspired this story. While I have not been able to know you up close and personal these many years, you are so dearly loved for who you are—my Princess granddaughter.

—Grandpa "B."

acknowledgments

● ▪ ● ▪ ● ▪ ● ▪ ● ▪ ●

I would like to thank the following people for their collaborative involvement in this book:

Dave Bellis, my friend and colleague for twenty-six years, for being one of my coauthors. Dave selected the content elements from *Beyond Belief to Convictions* and developed a storyline that would effectively communicate that content. While he wrote the content elements of the novel, the Ratsbane and "Inside Story" sections of the book, and collaborated with Bob Hostetler and me to complete the entire project, he requested that his name not appear on the front cover. He says he doesn't need the recognition since he doesn't aspire to author any books of his own, but I certainly recognize both his ownership of this message and his writing skills to help deliver this work to you.

Bob Hostetler for being my other coauthor. Bob labored through the collaborative process to generate a completed work with Dave. It is Bob's talent as a writer and novelist that brought this story to life on the printed page. His creativity and writing abilities are unsurpassed.

Lynn Vanderzalm of Tyndale House Publishers for applying her analytical skills and editorial expertise to this project. I have often said Lynn is more than an editor; she is a collaborative partner who is deeply committed to the biblical message we are proclaiming and dedicated to excellence in communicating that message.

Jennifer Stair for her excellent copyediting of the manuscript. Her speed, efficiency, and attention to detail made the manuscript a better book.

Josh McDowell

trouble in westcastle ch. 1

RYAN ORTIZ shimmied through the high, narrow bathroom window and dropped to the filthy tile floor below. "I'm in!" he breathed, just loud enough for the others outside to hear.

"Good." The voice belonged to Seth Holcomb, the three-sport star of Eisenhower High School's athletic teams.

"Don't turn any lights on!" warned Adam Warren, a linebacker for the Eisenhower Generals, the school's football team. Adam would have been too large to fit through the window, but that wasn't why Ryan had been selected to do the breaking and entering. The two athletes were only too happy to let Ryan do the dirty work.

"I won't," Ryan assured them in a whisper. He looked around the dim bathroom of the electronics store. The room wasn't much larger than a closet, and the odor of the enclosed place was nearly overpowering. He unconsciously wrinkled his nose. "I'll go find the alarm system."

"It should be by the back door," Seth said. "You still have the wire cutters?"

Ryan reached around to the hip pocket of his jeans and pulled out the wire cutters. "Yeah," he croaked. He suddenly realized how dry his throat was, and he admitted to himself that he was terrified. He shut his eyes for a moment and shook his head. *I can't believe I'm doing this,* he thought. He licked his lips, swallowed hard, and opened his eyes. He was facing the door.

He pulled his dad's old work gloves out of his other hip pocket and slipped them onto his hands before grasping the bathroom doorknob. He'd never done anything like this before, but he knew better than to leave fingerprints behind.

Once through the door and into the dark interior of the large Electronic Zone store, he peered around carefully, quickly orienting himself. He scanned the walls and ceiling. It looked like Seth had been right; there didn't seem to be any security cameras. He sighed with relief, turned toward the rear of the store, and walked toward the back door. Seth had been right again; the alarm system keypad hung on the wall next to the door.

"Guys!" he hissed through the door.

"Come on, Ortiz," Adam responded. "Open the door."

"Guys, there are no wires to cut!" he said.

There was no response for a moment and then Seth's voice answered. "Pull it away from the wall. Then cut the wires behind the thing."

Ryan licked his lips. Seth and Adam had made it sound so easy, but it wasn't working out that way. They'd made it sound like they could almost walk in, pick up hundreds of dollars' worth of computer devices, game consoles, and software, and walk out as easy as if they were ordering a Big Mac at the drive-through. But Ryan's hands were shaking now, and he continued to scold himself. *I can't believe I'm doing this,* he thought as he gripped the alarm system keypad and pried it off the wall.

He waited a few seconds for lights to begin flashing and sirens to go off. When that didn't happen, he inspected the dangling device in the dim light. Seth had said to cut the wires. He lifted the wire cutters. He hesitated.

"Are you sure this'll work?" he asked the jocks on the other side of the door. "What if it sets off the alarm?"

"Just do it and let us in!" Adam growled.

"Ortiz, don't choke now," Seth said. "If the alarm goes off, we can be out of here in seconds."

Ryan inhaled deeply. He didn't want to choke. He was supposed to be proving himself to these guys, showing them that he could run with them—not Adam, so much. Adam was just a 250-pound bully, a real jerk. But Seth—everybody at Eisenhower looked up to Seth, even the teachers.

"All right," Ryan said finally. "I'm doing it." He threaded the wires between the wire cutters and snipped them. Nothing happened. He hesitated just a moment, then he turned the deadbolt on the back door and swung it open.

Adam pushed immediately past him and into the store, but Seth stopped and clamped a hand on Ryan's shoulder. "Way to go, Ryan," he said.

Ryan watched Adam and Seth separate and begin working in the semidarkness of the store, filling large plastic garbage bags with computer games and accessories. He smiled; that was the first time he could remember Seth Holcomb calling him by his first name. Guys like Seth and Adam had always called him "Ortiz," never "Ryan." Hearing Seth use his first name signaled to Ryan that he had done it. They accepted him. He was one of them, one of the elite . . . like his older brother Tony had been. It had always come easily for Tony, who was a jock; but Ryan had always been better at math and science than football and basketball. Tonight, Ryan had finally proven himself.

"Ortiz!" Seth called. "Get to the front window! You're supposed to keep a lookout for us."

Ryan frowned. "Yeah," he said, nodding. "I'm there." He started toward the front of the store while the other two dragged their already-bulging bags along the floor. He positioned himself behind a display unit, at an angle from the plate-glass windows that formed the front of the store. He peered through the windows. The street seemed quiet, deserted . . . until a car turned off Monroe Street and started rolling slowly toward the store. Ryan watched it approach and then gazed back into the store to check on the progress of his new friends. He couldn't see much inside the store; his vision had adjusted to the better-lit street outside.

He turned his gaze to the street again, and his mouth dropped open. His chest felt like someone was squeezing him in an agonizingly slow Heimlich maneuver. The car was a police cruiser. He first saw the emergency light fixture atop the car, and then his eyes focused on the insignia on the doors. It crept slowly toward the store in silence, only its headlights piercing the darkness.

"Guys!" Ryan hissed.

There was no answer.

"Seth! Adam!" he called. "It's the police!"

Still no answer.

Ryan crouched down the store aisles to alert his friends, calling for them but trying to make as little noise as possible. He crept to the spot where he had last seen Seth, but there was no sign of him or Adam.

Oh, God, he said silently, not sure whether he was cursing or praying. *Oh, God, I can't believe I'm doing this. What if they catch us? What if we're arrested?* But he knew the answer. He would be charged with breaking and entering, and robbery—maybe grand theft, if they were caught with enough merchandise. If convicted, it would completely change his life. The scholarship to M.I.T. he'd been working toward for years—that would be history. All his hard work would go down the drain—just for the chance to be accepted by some of the most popular guys in school. He didn't have to ask himself if it was worth it. He knew, if he got caught, it wouldn't be worth it, not in a million years.

"Adam! Seth! Are you guys there?" Ryan continued to try to locate his friends, checking every aisle, until he reached the back door. He looked through the store again. They weren't there. He wondered how long they'd been gone.

He was seventeen years old, but he suddenly felt like crying. But he knew he couldn't; he *wouldn't*. He licked his lips, swallowed hard, and with a shaking hand, opened the back door and stepped out into the alley.

Instantly, the flash of lights and wail of a siren pierced the air. A police cruiser aimed its headlights at him and sped down the narrow alley. Reflexively, he ducked back into the store and slammed the door behind him, throwing the deadbolt. He was locked inside the store . . . alone.

▪▪▪▪▪▪▪▪▪▪▪

SIXTEEN-YEAR-OLD SARAH MILFORD finished her cheerleading routine with a perfect back handspring, faced the panel of judges, propped her hands on her hips, and winked, in unison with the last note of the song she had used to accompany her routine.

The lanky, pretty brunette had "nailed" her varsity cheerleading tryout, and she knew it. She'd been working on her cheer routine for almost a year, since failing her tryout for the squad during her freshman year. Jennifer Brown had made the team, though, and had spent the past year rubbing Sarah's nose in it. But that's how things had been between Sarah and Jennifer for years now.

The two girls had been good friends once, back in

third grade, when Jennifer's family had just moved to town. Sarah quickly befriended the new girl, and they became almost inseparable, even as Jennifer began to make other friends. But when Jennifer Brown and Jessica Furman discovered each other, Sarah suddenly found herself on the outside. Worse, "the J-Crew," as Jennifer and Jessica called themselves, seemed to take pride and pleasure in their ability to taunt and torture Sarah Milford, the preacher's daughter.

Sarah pulled a towel from her gym bag, wiped her face, and glanced over at the judges' table. Miss McPherson, the history teacher and cheerleading coach, sat between Jennifer Brown and Nina Fantana, the senior star of the cheerleading squad.

Suddenly Sarah's heart seemed to stop beating. Jennifer turned her head slowly as she talked and pinned her gaze on Sarah. Sarah could tell that Jennifer was talking about her, and the sneer on her face was a telltale sign that whatever she was saying wasn't good. Sarah looked at Miss McPherson's face; she was tight-lipped and seemed slightly annoyed with Jennifer. But Nina . . . .

Nina Fantana was nodding. She looked Sarah up and down, as though estimating her height. She seemed to be buying everything Jennifer was selling.

Sarah felt herself blush, not with embarrassment but with indignation. She wanted to walk up to the table, plant her hands on her hips, and say, "I was perfect. You know I was. You know I earned a spot on the squad." But she didn't. Instead, she waited and watched as Jennifer continued to talk. Miss McPherson spoke a couple of times, but she managed only a few words before Jennifer interrupted.

Finally, Sarah watched as the three judges each wrote in their notebooks. Jennifer started to rise from her seat, but Miss McPherson placed a hand on her arm, almost as if she were trying to physically keep Jennifer in her seat.

She shook her head, said a few curt words to Jennifer, and then stood and walked to Sarah.

Sarah tried to prepare herself as Miss McPherson approached, smiling halfheartedly.

"You did an excellent job on your routine," Miss McPherson started. "I'm very proud of you."

Sarah's eyes started to fill with tears. *Don't cry*, she told herself. *Don't you dare cry.* She glanced at the table. Jennifer watched, a wicked smile on her face. Sarah turned back to Miss McPherson. "I didn't make it," Sarah said. It wasn't a question.

Miss McPherson shook her head. "I'm sorry, sweetie," she said.

Sarah nodded, still fighting the tears. "Can you tell me why?" she asked, a note of defiance in her quivering voice.

Miss McPherson nodded slowly. "Your routine was perfect," she said.

Sarah bit her lip. She loved hearing that, but she knew the bad news was coming.

"But," the teacher continued, speaking very slowly, "the panel . . . thought your style would be a bit . . . tame . . . at least, compared to what they're looking for in the squad this year."

"Tame?" Sarah repeated.

"I'm sorry, sweetie."

"Isn't there something I . . ." Sarah didn't want to give up so easily. She'd worked so hard. "I mean, isn't there a way to . . . can I . . ."

Miss McPherson shook her head. "I'm afraid not. We only have a few slots available, and the panel's decision is final. There's not much else either one of us can do. But you should be very pleased with what you've accomplished. Very few girls can execute a routine the way you just did."

"Thanks," she said, without feeling. She turned from

the teacher and picked up her gym bag. She started to leave the large gymnasium. As she approached the exit, Jennifer stepped into her path.

"It's better this way," Jennifer said.

"Just let me go, Jen," Sarah said. "I don't feel like talking right now."

"No, but really, it's much better this way."

Sarah sighed. "Okay, Jen, whatever you say." She tried to step around Jen, but the other girl moved again to block her way.

"This way," she purred, "you only have to be humiliated once. If you had made the squad, you would have humiliated yourself over and over again."

Sarah felt her face flush. She suddenly felt unbelievably tired. It seemed to her like she worked and worked—to please her parents, her friends, the people at church, her teachers—and it was never good enough. Even when she executed a perfect cheer routine, it still wasn't good enough to make the squad. It would never be good enough, she thought; it seemed like she could never be good enough to get what she wanted: just a little acceptance, a feeling that someone—somewhere—thought she was good enough to be part of the group just the way she was.

Jen was still standing in front of her with a gleeful expression. Sarah wished she could say something clever, something that would put Jen in her place, but she couldn't think of anything. She simply stepped past Jen and pushed open the gym door. She held back the tears until she was in her car, alone.

⬛▪⬛▪⬛▪⬛▪▪⬛▪⬛

RYAN CRINGED in the dim store. He was trapped, and he knew it.

Suddenly he heard heavy banging on the door he had just locked, and a deep voice on the other side demanded,

"Police. Open the door!"

He looked up and down the aisles of the store, illuminated only by the streetlights outside the big plate-glass windows at the front. Adam and Seth had apparently escaped, probably with thousands of dollars' worth of stolen merchandise. He would be blamed for it all, and if he told the police who else was involved, he would be the most despised person at Eisenhower High School. And he could forget about scholarships and college and everything else.

He'd never been in trouble before. He wouldn't know how to act. He didn't know how to act now. But he knew one thing: He couldn't get in much deeper.

The banging on the door continued, and he suspected another cruiser would soon screech to a stop in the front, blocking all escape. He thought suddenly that an officer could even now be jogging to the front of the store. He had only one chance, he figured, and he had only seconds to take it.

He swallowed hard. He took a deep breath, exhaled, and then ran toward the windows at the front of the store. At the last minute, he leapt and rolled into the window, covering his face with his gloved hands as he shattered the glass and tumbled out onto the sidewalk. Immediately, he was on his feet and running as fast as he could down the street.

He turned down a side street just as he heard a siren behind him, approaching fast, with a squealing of wheels. But he ducked quickly into a dark doorway to catch his breath and heard the patrol car pass. Still shaking, he carefully brushed the glass fragments from his clothing, waited a few more moments, and then emerged from the doorway.

Ryan was still shaking when he arrived home twenty minutes later. His mother appeared before he even had time to close the front door.

"Where have you been?" she demanded.

Ryan looked at her. "Why?" He expected a couple grim-faced detectives to appear from the living room, like he'd seen a hundred times on television.

"That Seth Holcomb boy has called three times for you tonight," she answered. "Of all times for you to be out God-knows-where! He's such a nice boy, from a very nice family, and it's awfully nice of him to call."

"I know, Mom," he said. He turned toward the stairs and headed for his room.

"Well, are you going to call him? Your father and I have tried to tell you that you need to branch out, Ryan. It's not good to spend so much time alone in your room, even if it does get you grades and scholarships and what-not. There's no reason you can't make friends with people like Seth Holcomb and that Brady Fantana, boys like that." She was calling up the stairs, speaking to his back now. "Everybody knows you're a smart boy, Ryan. You just need to use your brains to fit in a little more."

Ryan paused at the top of the stairs and turned around to face his mother. He placed a hand on the banister to steady himself; he still hadn't stopped shaking. "I know, Mom," he said. "I'll try." He flashed her a weak smile and turned down the hallway to his room.

Once inside, he shut the door behind him and sat down on the bed. Almost immediately, however, he stood and paced the floor. *I can't believe I did that,* he thought. He licked his lips and swallowed.

They're gonna find out, he thought. *They're gonna figure it out somehow. What if the cops saw me when I stepped out the back door? What if the store had hidden cameras? What if they call me in for questioning? What if somebody saw me running away? What if someone recognizes me?*

He continued pacing, struggling to control his raging panic. His eyes darted around the room, as though he would find the answer to his vulnerable situation. His gaze settled on his desk, where a stack of applications to the colleges with the finest math and science programs in the country lay. Beside the applications, next to the receiver for his cordless phone, was a brightly colored brochure that Duane Cunningham, the gung-ho youth pastor at Westcastle Community Church, had shoved into his hand after school a week or two ago. Ryan had almost forgotten about it. He reached for it.

It was a brochure for the youth group's upcoming SWAT (Summit Wilderness Adventure Training) trip. Ryan wasn't really a member of the youth group, but he attended some of the fun things they did, like four-wheeling at Beech Meadows or the trip to the water park. He looked over the brochure carefully and saw that the trip started early *the next morning.* He reached for his phone and dialed the number on the brochure.

"Duane?" he said. He knew he'd need his parents' permission, but that would be no problem. Besides, first things first. He tried to sound casual. "This is Ryan Ortiz. Hey, I was just wondering . . . is it too late to sign up for the SWAT trip?"

§ ▪ § ▪ § ▪ § ▪ § ▪ §

SARAH CAME IN THE BACK DOOR of the house and tried to slip past the door of her father's study. She didn't want to talk to anybody, least of all her parents.

"Princess, is that you?" Pastor James Milford of Westcastle Community Church had an assortment of pet names for his daughter. She hated most of them.

She poked her head through the doorway. "Hi, Daddy," he said.

He stayed seated behind his cluttered desk, a pencil perched behind his ear. "Your mother asked me to remind you that you need to stay in tonight."

"No problem," she said emphatically. She might just stay in for the whole spring break. She started to head for her room but stopped. She stepped back into the doorway. "Why?" she asked. "What's tonight?"

Her father wore a blank look for a moment, and then he nodded with realization. "She said something about packing for the youth group trip."

Sarah's mouth dropped open for a moment. She'd been so focused on preparing for the cheerleading tryouts, she'd completely forgotten the SWAT trip.

"Oh, Daddy," she said mournfully. "Do I have to go?"

"Have to go? Princess, you wanted to go."

"I know, but I don't feel like going anymore."

Pastor Milford removed his glasses and set them gently on his desk. "I don't understand."

"Is there any way I can get out of it?"

"Sweetheart, the youth group's counting on you. You're an important part of this trip."

"But—"

"What would it look like if the pastor's daughter backed out at the last minute?"

Sarah's face wore the expression of a prisoner pleading for clemency.

"And besides," her father continued, "Duane and Liz are counting on you. You don't want to let them down, do you?"

"No," she said. "I guess not."

He stood and circled his desk. He met her in the doorway and pulled her to him in a gentle hug. "That's my girl. You'll do great once you get there. You are a Milford, after all. We always . . . "

" . . . give our best," she finished, though her heart wasn't in it.

"And then some," her father added, completing the familiar family motto.

They stood wordlessly for a few moments. Sarah had long accepted she was a Milford even though she knew she was an adopted child. James and Marjorie Milford may not have been her birth parents, but they were her real parents. Yet she still struggled at times to feel she was accepted for who she was without having to live up to someone's expectations. Sarah slipped gently from her father's grasp. "I'll start packing," she said.

far below westcastle, in a dark and dank subterranean classroom, a strange figure switched off a large video screen and then turned from it to spit a string of curses at his classroom full of students—ten rows of twisted, deformed demons of hell, each of them in specialized training to become a tormentor of children and young people.

Like all demons of hell, these possessed ugly mutant bodies—one of many cruel jokes perpetrated by their master, Satan, on the forlorn angels who had long ago rebelled with him and so lost their position, power, and beauty.

The instructor, whose name was Ratsbane, was imprisoned in the wart-covered body of a giant toad, topped with the oversized head of a carpenter ant. His bulbous eyes reflected his surroundings like convex mirrors made of obsidian. His every move was awkward, made difficult by the constant challenge of coordinating his grotesquely mismatched body and head.

Ratsbane had ascended to his teaching post at Brimstone University, hell's advanced teaching and training institution, because of his experience as an operator of the Prime-Evil Transducer (PET), his work on the ill-fated

Apple Project during his time in the Research and Intelligence Division (RAID), and by his constant backbiting and betrayal of more powerful and more intelligent demons.

He glared at his students with black, soulless eyes. "Your job," he croaked, his voice belching up from his toady chest and throat, "is pathetically simple—not that I expect any of you dismally deficient demons to understand it. But your job is to make humans miserable, to keep them from experiencing true happiness and meaning until it saps the joy out of their wretched lives."

A demon with a ferret body and a partially decayed fish head spoke up. "How do we do that?"

Another demon, this one with the nearly intact body of a badger but with duck feet on her hind legs, growled, "Fool! We do it by getting 'em to do bad things." She turned to face Ratsbane. "Right?"

"That, my moronic undergraduates, is part of it," Ratsbane answered. "We always like bad behavior, of course—and the worse their behavior is, the more miserable they become. But our tempting and tormenting has a purpose!"

Another demon, who exuded a foul smell—even to these spirits, accustomed as they were to the smell of salt, sulfur, and flame—spoke enthusiastically. "We poison their attitudes, that's what we do! We get these wretched human kids to adopt all sorts of twisted values."

Ratsbane stifled a yawn. "Again," he said, "that's part of it. But focusing on their values will have limited results, too." He stroked his ant chin with toady fingers. "The secret to a weed's growth is not the leaves, and not even the stalk—it's the root."

"Right!" someone said.

"What's that mean?" said another.

The badger with the duck feet spoke again. "So what's the root?"

"Their *beliefs*," Ratsbane croaked. "Our overarching

goal is to distort their *beliefs.* We've got to deceive them. We've got to get them to believe the wrong things and then everything else will fall into place, my maggot-infested inferiors."

"Huh?" asked the badger, who was called Furblight. "How is that?"

"Look, we've got the stats," Ratsbane explained. "For example, research shows that nearly all the kids who believe that premarital sex is okay have actually had sex!"

"Yeah," argued the malodorous demon, who was called, simply, Stench. "That's just because everybody's doing it."

"That's the lie we want them to believe," Ratsbane countered. "But research shows that roughly one in four eighteen-year-olds has had sex, so it's not even a majority of kids—not yet. We just try to make 'em *think* everyone's doing it. My point is, when we deceive kids into believing the wrong things they will live wrong and be miserable." He turned to charts on the wall and pointed a deformed finger. "Look, depending on what we can get 'em to believe, we can manipulate kids into becoming more likely to get drunk, steal, use illegal drugs, even—" his mandibles opened and closed as if he were smacking his lips at the thought—"attempt suicide!"

"It's as clear as the hideous nose on your face," Ratsbane concluded. "The miserable things these kids *do* come from what they *believe.* So your job—and mine—as demons of hell, is to aim our weapons at the place they'll do the most harm, and twist, warp, damage, deform, deface, distort, and disfigure their beliefs. Yet we must be cunning and deceptive so they don't know they have adopted distorted beliefs. That is why you are here—to learn from me how to become the Deceivers. Then we can turn our human prey into the miserable pawns of hell."

At that, the roomful of demons spontaneously erupted in a bizarre cheer of grunts, growls, and groans, punctuated with the sound of grinding and gnashing teeth.

■ ■.■ ■■.■ ■■.■ ■■.■

(the inside story)
a three–dimensional story

MOST BOOKS tell a story of one kind or another. Those books that tell a fictional story are called novels. Books that don't are considered nonfiction. But this book is different; the story it tells will have three dimensions, not just one.

It's called a NovelPlus, a concept created specifically for the Powerlink Chronicles (*Under Siege, The Love Killer, Truth Slayers,* and this book). As you've already discovered, you'll be reading about two young people named Ryan Ortiz and Sarah Milford. You'll also meet other members of the Westcastle Community Church youth group: youth pastors Duane and Liz Cunningham, Jason Withers, Alison Cheney, and others.

You've also met the demon Ratsbane and the under-demons he is training to become the Deceivers, whose mission is to distort the beliefs of a generation and prevent that generation—*your* generation—from experiencing true happiness and meaning in life. You'll see how these residents of the underworld are working to rob the Westcastle kids of what they crave—unconditional love and acceptance, a sense of belonging, completeness, as well as connectedness and fulfillment in life—things we all crave.

But these occasional glimpses into the corridors of hell will not only reveal what evil the forces of darkness are perpetrating on the Westcastle kids but also expose the strategy Satan is trying to use on you.

The third dimension of this book are sections called "The Inside Story," in which we will interrupt the fiction at key points and present important insights or explanations of things that are going on in the novel, helping you also to apply that understanding to similar things that happen in your life. You may be so interested to learn what happens next in the stories of Ryan and Sarah and their friends (and foes) that you will be tempted to scan or skip these sections. Doing that, however, will deprive you of the full benefit of this NovelPlus and may prevent you from learning how to resist and counter hell's diabolical plot.

For example, the facts Ratsbane cited in the last scene represent real research, performed among kids just like you. Every demon in hell knows that kids today face unprecedented pressure. Like kids across the nation, you are exposed to sexual temptation, school violence, alcohol, illegal drugs, and a variety of influences that threaten to rob you of happiness and meaning in life.

Of course, none of us intentionally sets out to be miserable in life and end up as a drug addict or rejected by society and placed in prison for life. On the contrary, your generation appears to be the most occupationally and educationally ambitious generation ever, and you possess a high degree of spiritual interest. Studies show that:

65% of today's young people want a close relationship with God;[1]

45% want to make a difference in the world;[2] and

73% consider having close personal friends as a high-priority goal for their future.[3]

Based on the research, if you had to summarize in one sentence what you and the rest of your generation want in life, you'd probably say, *We want a healthy, relationally meaningful life on earth and a home in heaven.* That's what all of us want, isn't it? But at times it seems so hard to make a healthy, relationally meaningful life an everyday reality. It's easy to dream about what we truly want in life, but it's hard to make those dreams into reality. That's because, too often, we don't see the connection between our current beliefs and our hopes and dreams for the future. What we need is to find a way to connect our hopes and dreams for happiness and meaning to how we think and behave in life.

You see, our behavior comes *from* something. Our attitudes and actions spring from our value system, and our value system is based on what we believe. In his book *Kingdom Education,* Christian educator Glen Schultz says, "At the foundation of a person's life, we find his beliefs. These beliefs shape his values, and his values drive his actions."[4] Glen illustrates this through a pyramid that graphically makes the point that our visible actions are a direct result of our beliefs and values (see diagram).[5]

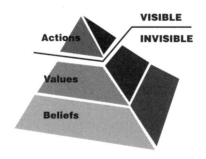

Research shows, like Ratsbane says, that kids who *believe* that premarital sex is morally right are far more likely to be sexually active.[6] Their beliefs shape their values, and their values lead them to exhibit specific attitudes and actions.

Research also shows that kids who don't have solid beliefs in Christianity are:

225% more likely to be angry with life;

218% more likely to be resentful;

210% more likely to lack purpose in life; and

200% more likely to be disappointed in life.[7]

Their beliefs create values that result not only in such harmful attitudes but also in specific behaviors. Again, what Ratsbane boasted about is actually supported by research, which has shown that kids who don't have solid Christian beliefs are:

200% more likely to steal;

200% more likely to physically hurt someone;

300% more likely to use illegal drugs; and

600% more likely to attempt suicide![8]

Our beliefs determine everything we do and define everything we become, which means that Ratsbane is right. If our enemy (and his demonic legions) can get us believing wrongly, then getting us to act wrongly will be much easier.

There is one belief that is especially critical in your life and mine, something very basic about Christianity that makes it real and relevant to you. And your enemy knows if he can deceive you in that key area, there will be little hope that you will ever experience true happiness and meaning in life. In fact, your enemy is probably trying to deceive you in that area right now, just as Ratsbane is going to try to do with Sarah and Ryan.

the swat
team

ch. 2

SARAH MILFORD reached into the back of Duane and Liz's sport-utility vehicle, dragged her backpack to the edge of the rear baggage area, and prepared to heave the heavy pack out of the vehicle. The six of them—Duane, Liz, Sarah, Ryan, Jason, and Alison—had left Westcastle early that morning and finally reached the trailhead, where their wilderness adventure was to begin, just before noon.

Suddenly Ryan Ortiz appeared beside her. "Let me give you a hand with that," he offered.

"I can get it," she said.

"No, really. You shouldn't—"

With a grunt, she yanked the pack out of the vehicle and threw it onto one shoulder. The pack seemed bigger than she was, but she held it there for a moment. A single strand of hair fell dangled from her forehead, and she looked at Ryan with a crooked smile. "I shouldn't what?"

"Nothing," he said. "I just thought—"

"Just because I'm a girl doesn't mean I can't carry my own pack."

"I know that," Ryan insisted. "That's not what I meant."

"Oh, okay, then," she said jauntily, as though she'd made her point. "I forgive you."

Ryan opened his mouth to speak, but Sarah tossed her hair back out of her face and turned away just as Duane Cunningham called for everyone's attention.

● ■.■ ● ■.● ● ■.■ ● ■.●

SARAH, Jason Withers, and Alison Cheney gathered around Duane and Liz in the small gravel parking area; Ryan stood by the SUV with a look of befuddlement for a moment, then shut the rear hatch of the vehicle and joined the others. He and Sarah had known each other for years, but they'd never been friends. They traveled in different circles and were both good students, but Sarah hung around the "religious" crowd, which Ryan had always figured was more or less what a pastor's daughter would do. Ryan had his own, small circle of friends, made up of a handful of guys who didn't fit into any of the standard cliques at Eisenhower High; they weren't jocks, scrubs, or freaks . . . and none of them played chess. He had hoped to change that, of course, and expand his circle of friendships to include Seth Holcomb and others. But he figured that plan was history now. He hadn't even called Seth back last night; the way Seth and Adam deserted him, he wished he never had to see them or speak to them again.

"We all know why we're here," Duane said. "This is called a SWAT trip." He unfolded a trail map and held it up. "We're starting here." He pointed to a circled point on the map. "So is the other team, the team we'll be competing against."

"Where are they?" Alison asked.

Duane and Liz shrugged in unison. Liz said, "Neither team is supposed to hit the trail until noon, so they may be coming anytime."

"We start from the same point?" Sarah asked.

Duane nodded. "Once we're all set, we'll be setting off into the Shiloh Wilderness with nothing except what we carry on our backs. We'll be hiking the Rock Creek Trail toward Shiloh Peak, stopping at two designated campsites along the way." He indicated their trail on the map and pointed to their campsites. Then he poked a finger at another spot on the map and continued. "The first team to make it—with every team member—to the summit of Shiloh Peak will capture the winner's flag that's already been planted there as part of our adventure.

"Now, the purpose of all this is to learn teamwork and leadership . . . and if we win, so much the better."

"Oh, we'll win," Sarah vowed.

The others turned to look at her. She blushed.

"I didn't mean to say that out loud," she said.

"But," Duane continued, "it's going to be more than just a fun wilderness adventure, because we're going to use this trip as an opportunity to get stronger and go higher in our faith as well, becoming more and more confident of the things we believe. So we'll be having devotions every morning and evening. Liz, Jason, and I will lead them."

"My devotions," Jason inserted, "will feature handsprings, back flips, and flaming batons."

"How are you gonna . . ." Alison started to ask and then quickly realized Jason was kidding. She blushed and giggled.

Ryan smiled and nodded at Jason's remark and Alison's reaction, but not before noticing that Sarah's expression had fallen suddenly when Jason said what he did.

"In addition to the devotions," Duane said, "we'll be

using some of our time on the trail to discuss the topics of each day's devotions. By the time the adventure is over, we're hoping that we'll be a better team, that each of us will have discovered some things about ourselves—and beliefs about God—that may very well change the rest of our lives."

Duane glanced at his watch just as a shiny luxury SUV screeched into the gravel parking area. The other team had arrived.

ratsbane lurched into the room on his gangly frog legs and discovered his demon students staring at the video screen while grimacing and gnashing their teeth. Furblight, the duck-footed badger demon, pointed at the screen. Her lip was curled in a vicious sneer. "Something must be done," she growled. "Something must be done."

Ratsbane advanced on her and slapped her fiercely with the back of his hand. "Seats!" he croaked.

The demonic classroom quickly retreated to their accustomed seating arrangement. When they were all in place, Ratsbane hobbled to Furblight's side and loomed over her. He tilted his head and fastened one great bulbous black eye on her.

"What were you watching?" he rasped out.

She eyed him warily and pointed again at the sophisticated video feed of the Westcastle youth group. "The older ones."

"Yes?" Ratsbane prompted. "What about them?"

"You should have heard what they said."

"What did they say?"

"They threatened—yes, that's what they did, they threatened the younger ones."

Ratsbane nodded and leaned toward her. "What did they threaten to do?"

Furblight looked around the room at the other demons, but none of them met her gaze. She looked back at Ratsbane and licked her snout with a long tongue. "They told the younger ones that they would discover some beliefs about the Enemy. They said they'd be having devotions every morning and evening."

She stopped, but Ratsbane said nothing. She saw only her own reflection in his glassy, obsidian eye.

"We've got to do something, right?" she asked, the fur on her neck bristling. "We've got to prevent them from believing, don't we? I mean, isn't that what you told us to do?"

"No!" Ratsbane shouted. He whirled so quickly that Furblight, thinking his sudden movement signaled another slap, recoiled, throwing herself out of her chair and onto the floor. Ratsbane ignored her, turning instead to the video screen. "No, no, no," he continued. "Write this down! Never strive to eliminate belief! It's an impossibility. Even the Lord Satan himself, the Prince of Darkness, as mighty and superior as he is, cannot prevent human souls from believing things. These human wretches are *constantly* believing something. They can't help themselves.

"As I told you before, our job is not to eliminate belief, not at all." He began pacing the front of the room like a general addressing his troops before an important battle. "We *want* them to believe, and we want to *keep* them believing. Our job is to deceive them into believing the wrong things—especially on one point. It is your DPD."

"It's your what?" muttered a demon near Ratsbane.

"Your DPD!" yelled Ratsbane. "The Deceivers' Prime Directive. Listen carefully. We must dupe these dopes into believing that they ought to rule their own lives and create their own way of experiencing happiness and meaning. That is your DPD, and it is your most potent weapon."

Silence reigned for a brief moment, until Furblight could no longer restrain herself. "How do we do that?" she asked.

Ratsbane grabbed a remote control from the desk and pointed it at the screen. Suddenly, Ryan's and Sarah's faces filled the screen in extreme close-up. "See these two kids?" he said. "They come from great families, as humans measure these things. They go to a good church. They do fine in school. But I've got them running around like rats in a rat maze, just like a million other kids. And I do it by concentrating my efforts where they'll do the most damage, and that is by keeping them focused on their own self-centered ways of creating happiness for themselves.

"Never—I repeat, never—do I let them experience the happiness and meaning the Enemy—curse his name!— wants for them. Never do I let them see how closely tied their happiness is to their relationship with the Enemy. Like a carrot on a stick, I keep them hungering and thirsting after happiness while simultaneously creating enough harmful attitudes and destructive behavior in their lives to rob them of the very thing they seek."

Immediately a dozen hands, paws, and claws shot into the air. Ratsbane had touched a nerve among the would-be tempters and tormentors. But just then a chorus of high-pitched shrieks and screams—as of souls being tortured—streamed from the public address system and pierced the heavy, putrid air, signaling that class had come to an end. The questions would have to wait.

∎ ▫ ● ∎ ▫ ● ∎ ▫ ● ∎ ▫ ●

(the inside story)
the great deception

THE DECEIVERS' Prime Directive hasn't changed since the beginning of creation.

Back in the Garden of Eden, God told the first couple not to eat of a certain fruit. But the evil serpent told Eve she didn't have to listen to God. He deceived her into believing she was perfectly capable of deciding for herself what was right for her. She thought she should decide whether the forbidden fruit was good for her or not. You know the rest of the story. Sin entered the world, Adam and Eve were cast out of the Garden, and every human born into the human race thereafter has suffered from the same deception.

At one point or another, most of us have bought into the idea that there are many ways to salvation. After all, no one has a corner on truth, right? And it seems pretty exclusive to say there is only one right way, doesn't it? It feels like it stifles our creativity and robs us of our freedom to determine what we think is best. In fact, research shows that a majority of your friends (and maybe you, as well) tend to think that way:

58% percent believe all religious faiths teach equally valid truths.[1]

65% percent believe there is "no way to tell which religion is true."[2]

63% percent believe Muslims, Buddhists, Christians, Jews and all other people pray to the same god, even though they use different names for their god.[3]

70% percent say there is no absolute moral truth.[4]

72% percent believe "you can tell if something is morally/ethically right for you by whether or not it works in your life."[5]

Be honest. Doesn't it only seem fair and right that you be given the right to say what you think is best for your own life? I mean, it's *your* life—you should know what's going to bring you happiness and meaning, right?

It's so easy to accept this way of thinking and living because it appeals to our desire to be ourselves, be free, respect others' choices, make our own choices while not judging others, and simply be given the chance to make it on our own.

Today most kids (like Sarah, Ryan, and Alison in our story) believe Christianity is one of their options to believe; if it works for them, it must be right . . . for *them*. That way of thinking says there are many ways to God and our job is to determine which one is right for us. There's just one problem with such a view: None of it is true.

- All religious faiths do not teach equally valid truths;
- there *is* a way to tell which religion is the true religion;
- Muslims, Buddhists, Christians and Jews do not pray to the same god;
- you cannot tell if something is morally/ethically right by whether it works in your life; and
- an absolute moral truth *does* in fact exist.

Still, most of us have been deceived into believing that *many ways are right, so everyone must create the way that is best for him or her.* There are at least three reasons that this is so.

First, the entire culture reinforces this view. Whether you realized it as it was happening or not, you have been taught for most of your life—at school, in movies and music, etc.—to be tolerant and not to be dogmatic. You've been culturally conditioned to believe that it is bigoted to claim that one group has the absolute truth to the exclusion of others.

Second, this line of thinking seems so reasonable on the surface. It "feels right" to most of us, because it appeals to your desire to create for yourself what works for you.

Third, most kids have never had the truth presented to them in a way that truly and attractively breaks through the deception.

That's exactly what we will try to do in this book: break through the deception. We will attempt to share the truth about these things as you've never before heard or seen it. And if you embrace it, we can guarantee you'll never again be the same.

But be warned. You have an enemy who will do all in his power to keep you from discovering the truth. He wants to keep you deceived, as you will see Ratsbane trying to do with the Westcastle youth group.

∎▪▪∎▪▪∎▪▪∎▪▪∎

THE OTHER TEAM'S SUV turned sharply, stirring up a cloud of dust and throwing gravel in the youth group's direction, and came to a sudden stop against the log parking barrier. As the Westcastle group looked on, the other team tumbled out and gathered at the rear of the vehicle.

Sarah recognized the driver first: Mr. Robinson, a man with two kids who attended Eisenhower High School. *Weird,* she thought, that someone on the other team would have kids from Eisenhower, too. She had hardly completed her thought when her gaze settled on the pretty blonde girl who was opening the rear hatch of the SUV: Jennifer Brown!

Sarah felt her face flush. *What is she doing here?* She watched in horror as Jennifer yanked a backpack out of the vehicle . . . and handed it to Jessica Furman. The whole scene seemed to unfold in slow motion. She watched Duane and Liz walk casually over to the vehicle; they each shook Mr. Robinson's hand and talked to the group as if they were normal people.

Sarah struggled to control her raging emotions. She couldn't believe that Jennifer and Jessica were on the team they'd be competing against. She was sure they'd find some way to ruin her whole trip, just as they'd ruined her tryout for the cheerleading squad.

᙮ ᙮ ᙮ ᙮ ᙮ ᙮ ᙮

RYAN WATCHED the other team's arrival with similar fascination, standing just a few feet behind Sarah. He, too, saw Mr. Robinson exit the driver's side of the SUV. He, too, recognized Mr. Robinson. But Ryan knew more about Mr. Robinson than the simple fact that his children attended school at Eisenhower. He also knew that Mr. Robinson was an officer of the Westcastle Police Department.

Ryan stared, trying to recall the events of last night. He thought back to those frightening moments in the store, the instant when he had stepped into the alley and had been caught in the glare of the police cruiser's headlights. Could Mr. Robinson have been one of those officers in the car? Was Ryan in danger of being discovered—way out here, miles and miles from home?

He shook his head and silently urged himself to calm down. He told himself it would be an unlikely coincidence. He tried to reassure himself that no one could have recognized him in that alley, as quickly as he dashed back into the store. He told himself that he had gotten away with it.

His calm quickly deserted him, however, when he focused his gaze again . . . on Mr. Robinson. He was standing beside Duane Cunningham, fastening his backpack strap across his chest and watching Ryan closely.

the search from within

ch. 3

SARAH SHOULDERED HER PACK, determined to forget Jennifer and Jessica and just make the best of this trip. She turned to Alison.

"Let's get started," she resolved.

Both teams were required to start their journey from the same trailhead, entering the wilderness at the same point. According to the map Duane had shown them, both teams' routes followed the same trail for about a half-mile into the woods before diverging into separate paths. Sarah and Alison asked Liz if they could lead the way, promising to wait for the rest of their team at the fork in the path, and Liz agreed.

"Are you okay?" Alison asked as they started out.

Sarah's head snapped to attention as though she had just been awakened from a dream. "What?" she asked, then she quickly realized what Alison had said. "Yeah, I'm fine. I just . . . I was surprised to see Jennifer and Jessica back there."

"Do you know them?" Alison asked.

"Yes, I know them," Sarah said. She pulled on her shoulder straps to change the pitch of her pack. "We don't get along too well."

Alison nodded, just as both girls were aware of voices behind them. They turned and saw Jennifer and Jessica a short distance away, talking and giggling as if they were totally unaware of anyone else on the path.

∎▪▪∎▪▪∎▪▪∎▪▪∎

RYAN FROZE in place and with great effort tore his gaze away from Mr. Robinson's eyes. He studied the ground in front of his feet as though expecting to read his rights there: *You have the right to remain silent.*

"Ryan," Jason said, clapping a hand on his teammate's shoulder. "You okay? You look like you're going to be sick."

Ryan glanced quickly at Jason but avoided his penetrating gaze. "Yeah," Ryan answered. "I was just thinking."

"I wouldn't know what that's like," Jason joked. He nodded toward the trailhead and Ryan, understanding Jason's unspoken invitation, joined him in starting out on their hike. They walked a few paces together before Jason picked up the conversation again. "What were you thinking about?"

Ryan was quiet for a few moments as they walked. Each of them occasionally adjusted his pack, getting used to the more than forty pounds of weight riding on their hips and tugging on their shoulders. Ryan knew if he told Jason what he was thinking about when he was avoiding Mr. Robinson's apparent scrutiny, he'd have to explain why he was so shaken by the presence of a Westcastle policeman on their SWAT trip. He had no desire, no intention, of telling anyone—least of all someone he looked up to as he did Jason Withers—about his stupid break-in at the Electronic Zone. There was just no way to explain it so Jason would understand. He didn't expect anyone to understand. He wasn't even sure he understood himself. But he knew, too, that he had to tell Jason something.

"Do you ever feel like you just don't fit in?" Ryan asked. "Anywhere?" He didn't look at Jason when he asked the question.

They walked on in silence for a few moments. "Yeah," Jason answered after a moment. "I do."

"Really." It wasn't a question, but a statement. Ryan found it hard to believe. Ryan was a couple of years younger than Jason, but Ryan knew that Jason had always been a popular kid at Eisenhower High. He couldn't imagine someone like Jason feeling the way he did: lonely, disconnected, inferior, unpopular.

They traveled further. The shaded trail they hiked was bounded by forest greenery on either side. The life in the forest seemed to pause to listen as Ryan and Jason approached.

"I just don't feel like I belong anywhere, I guess," Ryan continued. "I'm not a jock, I'm not a freak, I'm not anything really. I'm not saying I want to be like those people; I'd make an even bigger fool of myself if I went out for sports. And besides, I've never had much interest in sports or anything like that . . .

"I mean, I don't even know what it feels like to walk into a room and feel like I belong there, like people are glad to see me. Like I can relax and just be myself . . . and be accepted for who I am."

Jason nodded sympathetically. "I think everybody feels that way sometimes," he said.

Ryan looked at Jason without hesitating or breaking stride, an expression of intense pain on his face. "I feel that way *all* the time," he confessed.

§ ▪.▪ § ▪.▪ § ▪.▪ § ▪.▪

ALL CONVERSATION between Sarah and Alison ceased as they trudged along in front of Jennifer and Jessica for some distance along the trail. Sarah's irritation simmered silently, but Jennifer and Jessica chattered away energetically. Sarah blushed every time they laughed, sure that they were having fun at her expense.

It's so unfair, she complained to herself. *Girls like Jennifer can be so mean and hateful . . . how can they be so popular? Doesn't anyone see how they treat other people? I would never act like Jennifer; I'd be afraid everybody would hate me and think I was totally awful. But she and Jessica treat everybody else like dirt—even some of their own friends—and everyone else acts like they're the coolest.*

I get straight A's, I go to church, I do everything my parents tell me to do, and it's still not good enough. I know I practiced my cheer routine harder and longer than anybody, and it still wasn't good enough. If I do everything I can possibly do, and people still won't like me, what am I supposed to do?

Her eyes began to well with tears, when Alison interrupted her thoughts. "There's the fork," she said, pointing ahead.

Sarah quickly wiped her eyes and then turned to look back down the trail, past Jennifer and Jessica. She couldn't see the rest of their team. "We told them we'd wait here," she reminded Alison. She released the belt strap on her pack, shrugged it off her shoulders, and set it on the ground beside the trail.

Sarah watched Jennifer and Jessica start toward the opposite fork, then stop. Jessica waited while Jennifer sidled up to Sarah, an arrogant smirk on her face.

"I've got to give you credit," she said.

Sarah watched her warily, saying nothing.

"It's gonna be hard to lose twice in the same week—" she flipped her hair away from her face—"to the same girl." She spun around and walked back to Jessica. The two girls giggled to each other as they walked away, looking back occasionally, gloating, until their progress was hidden from Sarah and Alison by a bend in the trail.

"brilliant!" said furblight,

the badger demon with the webbed feet. The other demons were gone; she had lingered and groveled low before Ratsbane on the slimy classroom floor. "The others are dismally deficient, as you said. They are too dim-witted to see the brilliance of your plan."

Ratsbane leered at the crouching student demon. He had preyed upon many demons in the thousands of years he had spent as a resident of hell, but it had been too long since his last victim. Fur-covered flesh was far from his favorite—the fur caused terrible indigestion—but he sensed an ambition in this demon that would make her a pleasure to consume, fur or no fur.

"But unlike them, I see the beauty of your strategy, your malevolence." Her lips curled back to reveal a row of sharp teeth in a hideous, mirthless smile. "But . . . "

Ratsbane's lidless eyes bulged with suspicion. "But what?"

"Oh, your maliciousness, though I am not as clever as you, I can see why you would deceive humans into believing they rule their own reality and create their own happiness and meaning." She stood, balancing her fur-covered body on her spindly hind legs and webbed feet. "But I don't see that there's any greater advantage to that strategy as opposed to so many other crafty evils we could cultivate."

"You are so right," Ratsbane croaked.

"I am?" the badger demon responded quickly, her eyes glistening with surprise.

"Oh, yes. You are not as clever as I . . . not even close."

He lifted his toady hands toward her throat, as though preparing to strangle her, and then lowered them slowly. "Unfortunately, you are no worse than the other garbage the University sends to me. You see, my future fodder, what you don't realize is the thing that drives these humans, the thing they crave deep down inside."

He paused dramatically before continuing. "You see, the Enemy has designed them to crave meaningful relationships—especially with him."

"Meaningful relationships," Furblight repeated. "I don't understand."

"Of course you don't," Ratsbane answered. "It's been eons since any demon of hell has experienced even the shadow of a meaningful relationship. We can't even remember what it was like—therefore, we are poorly equipped to recognize it, much less avert it. But that's why *I am Ratsbane*," he boasted, thrusting out his slimy frog chest like a soldier in a review line, "and *you* are merely *Furblight*."

Furblight's lip curled again, this time not in a smile but in a bitter sneer.

"Meaningful relationships," Ratsbane continued, not noticing his subordinate's expression, "form a connection all humans crave, a connection that makes them feel like they belong. Meaningful relationships fulfill a longing placed deep within them by the Enemy himself, an irresistible longing to know and be known intimately. That intense craving to connect with someone else on a deep emotional level is the only way for them to experience true happiness and meaning. And it is beyond our capacity to explain."

"So why are you trying to explain it?" muttered Furblight.

"Because you don't have to understand something in order to kill it. But if you ignore or forget that human longing for meaningful relationships," yelled Ratsbane, "you'll never understand how to best keep them from having them!"

"Okay, okay," Furblight responded, cowering under Ratsbane's thunderous yelling.

"Now, as I was saying," Ratsbane stated after gaining his composure. "Deep within these pathetic humans is this yearning for someone to discover the real person inside and to love and accept them for who they are."

Furblight's eyes widened with amazement and horror. "That's horrible!"

"Yes!" Ratsbane answered. "Which is why we must prevent it at all costs. If we keep them believing they are the source of their own happiness and meaning, they will keep trying and trying to find a meaningful relationship in their own ways. But they will never find them."

"Never?" asked Furblight.

"Never!" Ratsbane immediately snapped. "That's because the ultimate source of meaningful relationships resides in a relationship with the Enemy . . . and in him alone. So let me repeat it: We can keep humans from making a relational connection with the Enemy as long as they keep believing they can—and should—create their own way of experiencing happiness and meaning."

Without thinking, Furblight clapped her paws together in fiendish glee. "Bravo!" she said. "Bravo!"

"So," Ratsbane concluded, "the whole time we're doing that, they're becoming more desperate, more lonely, more disconnected, more miserable. And those are the very emotions we can use to make kids like these West-castle vermin do unspeakable things to themselves and to others."

Furblight licked her snout with a dusky tongue. "That sounds delicious," she said.

"Oh, it is," Ratsbane croaked. "Because the lonelier and more miserable they become, the more likely they are to give up or give in to our temptations . . . and we can have our way in their poor, pathetic lives."

"Can I help?" Furblight pleaded, like a toddler begging for a cookie.

"Yes, you can, my anxious little hairball," he answered dismissively. "I will give you some hands-on —er, paws-on—training, and let you have your fun. But always remember: I am the teacher; you are the student. If you forget how to grovel, I'll soon be licking your bones like a Thanksgiving turkey."

$$\blacksquare\:\blacksquare\:\blacksquare\:\blacksquare\:\blacksquare\:\blacksquare\:\blacksquare\:\blacksquare\:\blacksquare$$

(the inside story)
the source of meaningful relationships

RATSBANE IS RIGHT. Deep down inside, we all crave meaningful relationships. We all desire to be wanted and needed and cherished as a valuable person. We all know what it's like to feel *un*accepted, *un*loved, *un*popular and *un*important. We desperately want a relationship with someone who looks beyond our failures and imperfections and loves and accepts us for who we are . . . even if we ourselves haven't quite figured out who we are.

Yet most people don't understand what makes relationships meaningful in the first place. Meaningful relationships exist because God exists. Ultimately, everything you and I want in life—all the things that bring relational happiness and meaning (love, acceptance, belonging, fulfillment, completeness, etc.)—owe their existence to God. Everything that is of value and of worth comes from him. The Bible says, "Whatever is good and perfect comes to us from God above" (James 1:17).

Life itself is even related to and dependent upon God

(John 1:4; Acts 17:25). The further God is relationally removed from the scene of human existence, the more anger, strife, and evil we have in the world. And, ultimately, a life without God leads to death.

Of course, most people today don't believe those things we've just stated. Most people in your generation don't believe that God is the ultimate and absolute source for everyone and everything. The majority of people think he exists, but they don't believe he has prescribed one true way for people to find happiness and meaning in life. They think he has left it up to us to create for ourselves what we think is best for our lives. And, they reason, if we choose wisely and our good deeds outweigh our bad deeds, then we'll be able to go to heaven. In fact, 84% of church-attending kids in your generation believe just that way.[1]

But it is just that kind of believing that makes you over 200% more likely to be resentful, lack purpose, be angry and disappointed in life, and 600% more likely to attempt suicide. It's not hard to understand. The more we believe that relational happiness and meaning in life are something we create, the less we will look to a relationship with God for that happiness and meaning. The more we think we are to decide what's best for us, the less we'll follow God's way and believe that it's best for us. And the further removed we get from the very relational source of true happiness and meaning, the less happiness and meaning we'll experience in life.

God is the ultimate source of meaningful relationships. The truth is, by forming a meaningful relationship with him you and I can begin experiencing the kind of happiness and meaning God intended for us. But that truth is exactly what Ratsbane wants to distort and twist and keep confused in the minds and hearts of Sarah, Ryan, Alison . . . and all of us.

∎▪●∎▪●∎▪●∎▪●

SARAH DROVE her last tent stake into the soil at the Westcastle team's first campsite. They had reached the clearing less than thirty minutes earlier and had immediately set to work. Dusk was approaching rapidly, Duane and Liz explained, and it was important that they set up camp as completely as possible while daylight remained. The campsite comprised a wide circle of level ground, blanketed with pine needles, and a fire-blackened ring of rocks in the center. The brisk waters of Rock Creek flowed nearby, providing the necessary water source for an ideal campsite.

Sarah and Alison each tied back their tent flaps and looked proudly at their handiwork. Sarah turned around and saw Jason and Ryan still busily staking their tent.

She hoisted her backpack into the air and hung it from a low branch of a tree, as the group had been instructed to do to keep bears and other animals from raiding their food stores. Then she nodded to Alison and strolled across the clearing to join Jason and Ryan.

"Let me give you a hand with that," she said, snatching three tent stakes from the ground where Ryan knelt.

"What are you—" Ryan said, stopping when he spied the smirk on Sarah's face. He looked past her to Alison, who watched. His gaze settled on the girls' tent. "You didn't tell me it was a race."

She knelt in the soft soil and drove a stake through a tent loop with her bare hand. "It's not," she answered. "You just looked like you needed help." She smiled smugly at him for a moment and then turned slightly to focus on the trail into the campsite. Her jaw slackened and she stared, gape-mouthed.

"What's wrong?" Ryan asked.

Sarah pointed, unblinking, as if she couldn't believe her own eyes. Jennifer Brown and Jessica Furman hiked toward them.

a man
named eli

ch. 4

A BEARDED MAN with a slight limp trailed Jennifer and Jessica into the Westcastle team's campsite. Sarah watched in stunned silence as the man introduced himself to Duane and Liz as Eli. He said he'd been a ranger in that wilderness for more than twenty-five years and supposed that he knew it as well as anyone.

"I came across these two young women on the banks of Whitetail Creek," Eli explained. He spoke slowly but clearly, his voice ringing with authority. He wore jeans and hiking boots, with a simple brown shirt that was slightly frayed at the collar. Strapped to his back was a well-worn canvas knapsack, a third of the size of their backpacks. "They'd apparently gotten a little disoriented and didn't know which way to go. That's easy to do in the wild."

Jennifer and Jessica still hadn't spoken. They looked around the campsite without meeting anyone's eyes and seemed to be inspecting the scene.

"So," he concluded, as though he had explained

everything, "here they are."

He looked from Duane to Liz and then glanced briefly at Jason, Ryan, Sarah, and Alison. Finally he turned his gaze back to Duane. "Something wrong?" he asked.

Duane ran a hand through his sandy hair. "It's just that, well—"

"This isn't our campsite," Jennifer interrupted. Her voice dripped with annoyance. "This is the team we're competing against."

Eli nodded slowly. "That explains why there were only three tents," he said, glancing at Ryan and Jason's tent, which still lay flat on the ground. "And why you all didn't jump for joy when we walked into camp."

Jump for joy? Sarah thought. *Yeah, right.*

Duane nodded back at Eli. "I'm afraid she's right. These ladies belong to the other group that's heading up to Shiloh Peak. It's a wilderness competition; first group to the Peak on the third day wins."

"Third day?" Eli echoed. "That'll take some hiking."

Sarah spoke up as a pleasant thought occurred to her for the first time since Jennifer and Jessica had appeared. "But it only counts if the whole team makes it together." She glanced quickly at Jennifer and was rewarded with an angry glare. She could see that Jennifer already knew what Sarah had just realized: by getting lost, Jennifer and Jessica had caused their team to lose precious time in the race to Shiloh Peak.

"We all started from the same trailhead," Liz said, "but their group took the right fork."

"Well," Eli said. "I'm as sorry as I can be." He faced Jennifer and Jessica. "I assumed from where I found you that you'd strayed from this trail. I don't know how you ever got on the west bank of Whitetail Creek from where you started."

"Your team must be worried sick about you," Liz said. Eli gripped the two-way radio clipped on his belt.

"I'm sure they are. I'll try to call the base station and see if they can get word to your party. I believe I know where they'll be camping tonight—unless they're out beating the bushes looking for you two. If they are, of course, that's all the more reason to get word to them; they'll want to know you're all right."

Jessica blushed, but Jennifer seemed unfazed by the possibility that her whole team could be wandering around in the dark calling their names.

He lifted the radio to his ear, but Jennifer interrupted him. "Can't you just take us back?" she asked.

Eli shook his head. "Afraid not. That campsite is two hours away," he said, "and it's dusk already. Night falls fast in the woods, and it's just plain foolish to hike at night unless you have to. Too much can go wrong on the trail in the dark."

"What are we supposed to do?" Jennifer asked, panic rising in her voice. She was starting to sound like a petulant child who was used to getting her own way.

Eli cocked his head and shot an expectant glance at Duane and Liz. "Looks like you've got three guests for the night. If that's all right." When they assured him it was, he shrugged off his knapsack and set it on the ground. Then he turned his attention back to the girls. "Nothing else to be done. I'll guide you back to your party first thing in the morning." Jennifer and Jessica just gazed at him, slack-jawed. "Might as well get that weight off your back," he suggested, helping the girls shed their backpacks.

Sarah looked from Eli to Duane, incredulous. The "J-Crew" would be spending the night.

▪ ▫ ▪ ▪ ▫ ▪ ▫ ▪ ▪ ▫ ▪ ▪

RYAN had said nothing during the whole exchange. He stayed by the tent he and Jason had abandoned when Eli and the girls entered the camp and watched the proceedings with interest. He knew Jennifer and Jessica from

Eisenhower High, of course, but they'd never paid any attention to him at school . . . or anywhere. They were in a different league from him, he'd always told himself, usually adding that he wasn't even playing the same game.

His thoughts strayed from the girls, however, when Eli picked the two-way radio off his belt. His heart suddenly leaped into his throat.

"He's got a radio," he said.

Jason looked briefly at Ryan. "Yeah," he said. "Why?"

Ryan glanced quickly at Jason. He hadn't meant to start a conversation. "Nothing," he said. "I just . . . I thought we were supposed to be cut off from the outside world, that's all."

"We are," Jason said. "Except, when something like this happens, I don't think it's breaking the rules or anything for him to have somebody notify the other team that the girls are here, you know? I mean, the girls' getting lost has probably put them way behind already, and it's not like he's helping them catch up or anything. If he didn't call, somebody could get hurt looking for these girls."

"Yeah," Ryan agreed easily. He was happy to let Jason think his concern was for the fairness of contest. But that wasn't what scared him about Eli's radio. As he watched the old ranger calling the base camp, he realized that—for all the distance he'd traveled—he was only a radio transmission and a phone call away from the Westcastle police. He was thinking he'd totally wasted his efforts; he was no safer here than he had been back home. Maybe even less, because he had no way of knowing what was going on with Adam and Seth. For all he knew, they could have been arrested by now. They could be telling the police that it was Ryan who'd broken in through the store's bathroom window. They could even be lying about him—saying that it was all Ryan's idea, for example—to save their own necks. If they were, his decision to leave town the day after the break-in was looking worse and worse by the minute.

He suddenly felt like his stomach was full of rocks. "I'm going to finish putting up our tent," he told Jason.

❦ ❦ ❦ ❦ ❦

SARAH turned to Alison. "What are we going to do?" she whispered.

"Well," Alison answered casually, "I think we're going to eat, and then—remember?—Duane said we'll have devotions around the campfire, and—"

"No," Sarah interrupted. "I mean about *them!*"

"Oh," Alison said, shifting her gaze to Jennifer and Jessica, who huddled together across the campsite, apparently talking about something important. "I see what you mean. I guess we should offer them our tent, huh?"

"No!" Sarah said. "Are you crazy?"

"Well—"

"You don't know these girls like I do, Alison. They can't sleep in our tent."

"Well, they can't sleep with the boys!"

Sarah rolled her eyes. "I know," she said.

"I think it would be nice if we did something to make them feel welcome," Alison suggested.

Sarah sighed, amazed that even way out here in the middle of nowhere, Jennifer Brown still managed to make things difficult for her. Suddenly she had an idea. "Come on," she said, gripping Alison's arm and dragging her along with her.

Liz and Duane stood talking to Eli; they seemed to be discussing the plan for the evening when Sarah and Alison approached.

Sarah waited for them all to look at her. "Alison and I were just talking," she said. "Liz, what if you slept with Alison and me tonight, and Duane slept with Ryan and Jason? That way, Jennifer and Jessica could have a tent all to themselves."

Duane and Liz looked tentatively at Sarah for a moment after she finished speaking. Alison looked surprised at first and then smiled broadly.

Liz spoke first. "That would be fine," she said, "except that Eli needs a place to sleep, too."

"I've got a bedroll in my knapsack," Eli announced. "I'll be fine by the fire."

Sarah clapped her hands, her mission accomplished, when Jennifer suddenly spoke from over her shoulder.

"I don't mean to interrupt," she said, "but we caused all this trouble by getting lost in the first place. We don't want to make things worse by making people give up their tents or anything like that. We think we should be the ones to sleep out here."

Sarah's eyes narrowed. They were actually being nice. What was that about?

"It gets really cold at night here," Eli warned. "Have you ever slept out of cover in the woods?"

"No," Jennifer admitted. "But really, we feel awful as it is. We'd just feel that much worse if we caused any more problems."

Eli, Duane, and Liz still seemed hesitant.

"Please?" Jennifer added sweetly.

Duane broke the impasse. "Eli, you could share my tent, and Liz can triple up with Sarah and Alison. If you think the girls will be okay out here."

"We'll have the fire to keep us warm," Jennifer offered.

"That's *so* nice," Alison cooed.

Eli shrugged. "I reckon it's all right, then."

Sarah saw Jennifer and Jessica exchange satisfied smiles. They wouldn't be sharing her tent, but she was sure they were figuring out some new way to make her life miserable.

■ ■ ● ■ ■ ● ■ ■ ● ■ ■ ●

ELI, Jennifer, and Jessica joined the Westcastle group for a hot meal around the campfire, their first since entering the trail that morning. Lunch had been a cold meal each individual had pulled from his or her backpack; some had crackers and peanut butter, others whipped up a simple tuna salad, and Jason Withers had crowed about his "Jerky Burrito Supreme" concoction. But the evening meal of noodles and instant potatoes each person mixed in a large plastic cup of hot water satisfied the famished campers more than the fanciest fare back home.

When the meal was over and everyone had rinsed the utensils and cups by the stream, Liz called everyone to gather around the campfire for their first nightly devotions. She explained to the three guests what they were doing and invited Eli, Jennifer, and Jessica to participate as much or as little as they liked.

Jason stepped forward with a trail guitar, an oddly shaped acoustic instrument, smaller than a normal guitar. He led the group in a time of singing and prayer and then nodded at Duane.

"I know our guests may not be overjoyed to be spending the night with us," Duane said, nodding to Eli, Jennifer, and Jessica, "but I'm glad you're here." He thanked them for participating in the devotional period and continued. "I want to start our devotional times this week by pointing out that what happened earlier today to Jennifer and Jessica has happened to all of us.

"Whether we know it or not, we have all gotten lost on the trail. We have all lost our way and so lost the ability to find true happiness and real meaning in life. We are separated from God, relationally disconnected from him—and from each other. We're all wandering aimlessly, alone and with no real understanding of who we are.

"But God never wanted us to be relationally disconnected from him. He never wanted us to be separated from the source of happiness. His design for us is a life like the one enjoyed by the first man and woman. In the beginning moments of their existence, Adam and Eve lived in a pristine, flowering garden, a world that was theirs to keep and tend, a land where they lived in perfect harmony with each other and with their Creator, as a Father and as a friend. And that relationship—more than all the fruit-bearing trees, more than all the crystal waters, more than the perfect beauty and comfort of their surroundings—provided everything their human hearts desired. They had unconditional love and acceptance because their love and acceptance came from God. They had total joy because their joy came from God. They had perfect peace because their peace came from God. There was no hunger or fear, no anger or pain, because they enjoyed a perfect relationship with God."

Only the crackling of the fire and the gentle babble of the nearby stream accompanied the sound of Duane's voice. He paused, and Ryan looked around at the other faces in the circle. Everyone—including their guests—seemed to be as interested in what Duane was saying as Ryan was.

"You know the story, of course," Duane continued. "Adam and Eve sinned, and their sin drove life from the world and severed their connection to the holy presence of God. Gone were Adam and Eve's shared moments of intimacy and happiness with their Father God. Gone were the thrills of laughter they enjoyed together. Gone was their close relationship. 'From that moment on, sin and death reigned over every human born into this world' . . . including you. Yet even in the Garden, God knew how he would respond. Even before the world was created, he devised a masterful and merciful plan, a plan by which he would not only find you, lost and alone on the trail, but also make it possible for you to be relationally reunited with him and thus supply you with the right relationship your life has been missing."

"make it stop!

Make it stop!" Stench, the foul-smelling demon who most resembled a bear, covered his eyes with his fists.

The classroom video monitor was trained on the Westcastle group's campfire scene, and Ratsbane peered at his classroom of demons with undisguised malice. He seemed to take pleasure in Stench's distress.

"Why are you just standing there?" Furblight protested. She pointed a long claw at the monitor. "They're telling those kids all about how God—er, the Enemy—wants a right relationship with them, and . . ." She stopped, hacked loudly, and spit out a glob of yellow-green substance onto the floor. "You've got to do something!" she demanded.

Ratsbane hungrily scanned the roomful of evil spirits. "Why?" he asked.

"Why?" Furblight echoed. "Why? Because . . . because he's telling them all about . . ." She looked around the room as though afraid to speak the words. She finally leaned closer to Ratsbane and whispered, "*you know what!*"

"Silence!" Ratsbane croaked. "You totally miss the point. It's okay for them to hear the same old story of 'God so loved—'"

Stench gasped audibly. "*No!*" he screamed, as though he had just been stabbed. "Say it ain't so!"

"It *is* so," Ratsbane said, "*if* it's the same ol' same ol'; hell's not too scared of that. What's dangerous about what's going on up there is that my old nemesis Duane is making it fresh and new to those kids. He's beginning to connect the dots between a right relationship with God and their own pathetic need for happiness and meaning in their lives." He peered at Duane's image on the screen. "That's what makes this one so dangerous . . . but I'm not finished with these kids yet."

* * * * * * * * * *

RYAN was no longer looking at Duane. He'd been listening intently, but his eyes gazed into the fire. As Duane talked, it was almost as if Ryan could see the scenes he described portrayed in the dancing flames and flickering light of the campfire. When Duane talked about Adam and Eve's sin, however, Ryan saw not a garden and a serpent, but his own narrow escape from the electronics store.

Ryan knew in his mind and felt in his heart that Duane was describing him. He had been lost, wandering, alone. And though he'd known it all along, he suddenly realized completely that his little escapade with Seth and Adam had just been a stumbling attempt to be accepted, to find something that would make him feel like he really belonged. But it hadn't done that. Not even close.

What was I thinking? he asked himself. *How could I have thought Seth and Adam would ever have really accepted me? I mean, even Sarah thinks I'm weird, and she gets along with everybody.*

He rotated his head slowly and watched Sarah for a few moments. She seemed totally absorbed in what Duane was saying. She was beautiful, of course, but that was only part of what Ryan saw in her face; he saw something different in her, something that was lacking in most other girls, even those—like Jennifer and Jessica—who might otherwise have been just as pretty as Sarah. In spite of the teasing she'd thrown at him earlier, he couldn't see any flaw in Sarah Milford.

It's me, he concluded. *There's something wrong with me,*

and I guess I should just get used to that.

His gaze returned to the flames, and his thoughts once again returned to what Duane was saying. "Imagine how God felt as he watched you being born into the world he created for you," Duane continued. "It was the world where he and Adam once walked in perfect relationship with each other. Even before you drew your first breath, he longed to relate to you as intimately as he once did with Adam and Eve. He wants you to experience the true happiness and meaning in life that is found only in a relationship with him. But like all human beings, you have been trying to create your own happiness and meaning outside of him."

Duane turned and looked into the campfire and said nothing more. Thirty seconds passed. Those sitting around the fire looked at each other, wondering if Duane was finished.

"Are you done, honey?" Liz said, breaking the silence.

"Not quite," Duane responded still looking into the fire.

"I know all of you have heard these things before," he stated slowly. "So much so, they seem like fairytale stories. But on this trip I'd like to explain something different about our relationship with God. I want you to really believe that God wants a relationship with you, but not just any kind of relationship. He wants a relationship in which you are absolutely convinced that he is who he said he is, so that he can be to you what he said he'd be." Duane stirred the fire with a stick as he spoke.

"That may not make sense to you right now, but it's what I want to explain later. I'm praying that each of you will have a real encounter with the one true God of Abraham, Isaac, and Jacob, an encounter that will forever change your life. Would you like that?"

Duane finally looked up at the group as heads began

to slowly nod. "Okay, that's what we'll do," Duane said softly.

The atmosphere was subdued. Only the crackling of the fire could be heard. The first to move was Jason as he reached for his guitar. He began to softly strum a familiar worship song. Before long, Sarah, Alison, and Ryan united their voices with Jason's soft singing.

∎ ∎ ▪ ∎ ∎ ▪ ∎ ∎ ▪ ∎ ∎ ▪ ∎

(the inside story)
what we think a relationship is

DUANE IS ABOUT TO explain the kind of meaningful relationship God wants to have with the Westcastle group, and with all of us. It is going to be different from what Sarah, Ryan, and Alison have understood before. Oh, they have understood that God wants a relationship with them, just as you may have. But Duane is going to explain something new. They, like most of us, think God wants a relationship with us so we will obey him, follow him, and do good things. But that's not *why* God wants a relationship with us.

Duane is about to reveal the real truth about God's kind of relationship. But like you and me, the Westcastle group will have a hard time grasping what he says, because we have some distorted views of relationships. And these distorted views hinder us from experiencing the kind of relationship God wants to have with us—one that will result in true happiness and meaning.

Most of us pursue relationships in one of three ways. For example, Sarah longs to be wanted and needed, like all of us. She wants to be accepted and liked by others. She wants to be applauded for the things she accomplishes. But she believes that in order to achieve those things in her relationships, she must *perform*.

In a performing relationship, you have to do something to earn the other person's love, approval, and acceptance. Though it's often unspoken, this kind of relationship fosters the belief: "You will be loved and accepted

> "... *if* you get good grades."
>
> "... *if* you meet my expectations."
>
> "... *if* you don't embarrass me."
>
> "... *if* you don't strike out."
>
> "... *if* you meet my needs."

Things are fine in a relationship that is based on performance—as long as certain conditions are met. But sooner or later, our performance will suffer, since none of us is perfect. And when that happens, the happiness and satisfaction we long for—and performed so hard to find—slips away. As Sarah is learning, she can never be good enough to get the love and acceptance she wants. And whatever momentary acceptance or appreciation she gets is actually less meaningful because she knows it's conditional.

Ryan, on the other hand, tried another tactic. He's been trying to find happiness and meaning, too, but not by performing. He's been thinking that he can find satisfying relationships if he will only *conform*.

In this kind of relationship, you still have to do something to earn the relationship, but it's not awarded as a result of excelling or performing or setting yourself apart from other people; it's given in exchange for being *like* other people and conforming to a certain group or set of expectations. This way of relating to other people makes

you tend to believe: "You will find a sense of love, acceptance, and belonging

> **". . . because you dress a certain way."**
> **". . . because you like the same people
> I like."**
> **". . . because you hate the same people I
> hate."**
> **". . . because you talk a certain way."**
> **". . . because you do what I do."**

When you pursue relationships that are based on
conformity to certain customs or expectations, things will
be just fine—as long as you continue to conform. But if
you sit at the wrong lunch table or are seen with the wrong
people, the relationship may screech to a sudden stop.
This kind of relationship is ultimately unsatisfying, too,
because it never meets a person's deepest longing for a
relationship with someone who looks beyond our failures
and imperfections and loves and accepts us for who
we are.

Alison's approach to relationships is a little different.
She's not thinking she has to perform or conform in order
to find meaningful relationships. She believes she has to
reform.

Alison's approach to relationships is built on the
belief that people will love her and accept her as long as
she is *nice.* If she steps on someone's toes or bumps into
someone in the school hallway, she's so *sorry* . . . and determined to do better. She's trying as hard as Ryan and Sarah,
but her chosen method—like many of us—is to get better
and better at following all the rules and staying on everyone's "good side." Unfortunately, her attempts often fall
flat and leave her wondering why someone as nice as she
is still feels so hungry for close relationships. This

approach to relationships encourages the belief: "You will find a sense of love, acceptance, and belonging

> **". . . as long as you're as good as you can be."**
>
> **". . . as long as you're nice to everyone."**
>
> **". . . as long as you try hard to get along with others."**
>
> **". . . as long as you 'color inside the lines'."**
>
> **". . . as long as you follow all the rules."**

Relationships that are built on reforming your conduct to make others like you work okay—as long as you continue to reform. But like the other types of relationships, this approach is a dead end, too, because none of us can please everybody. No matter how hard we try, and no matter how we try to reform our personality or character, we're going to be disappointed, because a relationship built on reform will never meet our need for true happiness and satisfaction. Sooner or later, we'll realize that we're loved and accepted not for who we are, but for who we're pretending—or aspiring—to be.

Happily, none of these approaches is God's idea of a right relationship, which is why they will never bring true happiness and meaning for Sarah, Ryan, Alison—or you. And, of course, Ratsbane wants to keep it that way.

■ ■ ● ■ ■ ● ■ ■ ● ■ ■ ● ■

THE SOFT SINGING around the campfire eventually came to an end, and the group began to prepare for sleep. Duane and Liz were the first to gather their toothbrushes, wash kits, and water bottles for their evening ritual. As Ryan prepared to head to the stream to fill his water bottle, he stopped. Sarah stood by her tent, watching Alison wrestle around inside the tent to make room for Liz to join them for the night. His reverie was interrupted by a voice behind him.

"Take it easy, Romeo," Jennifer Brown said. "If you stare any harder at Milford, you're gonna bust a blood vessel in your eyeball."

Ryan's head snapped around. Jennifer and Jessica smiled mockingly at him, and even Eli stopped what he was doing to survey the scene. Ryan's face felt like it was on fire with embarrassment. He hesitated only a moment, then he strode to the path without a word.

He and Jason passed each other on the short path to the stream, and Ryan arrived there alone. He knelt on the bank, uncapped his bottle, and dipped it in the cold, rushing water. It was full in an instant. He capped it again and sat on a rock by the stream, unwilling to return to camp.

He turned and looked back up the path, as though he expected Jennifer to pursue him so she could taunt him some more. *How could I be so obvious?* he thought. *Jennifer must have been waiting for the chance to humiliate me like that. I should have said something to her. I don't know what, but anything would have been better than just walking away like that.*

"Hello, by the creek." It was Eli's voice.

Ryan turned. The old man trod softly along the path toward him. Ryan quickly grasped Eli's trail wisdom; he had called out to him from a distance to avoid startling him by approaching too closely or too suddenly in the dark.

"Hi," Ryan said simply, as Eli crouched by the creek to fill his own water bottle. He watched the man. Eli possessed the easygoing air of someone who is perfectly at home in the wilderness.

Eli spoke without turning to face Ryan. "It's no shame to like someone," he said.

Ryan nodded but said nothing. He didn't expect anyone to understand how he felt—certainly not someone Eli's age.

Eli finished his business and then stood and walked to where Ryan sat.

"The girl you were watching," Eli said, and Ryan sighed with discomfort. "Did I hear right? Her name is Milford?"

Ryan lifted his head and met Eli's gaze. He nodded. "Yeah," he answered.

"Sarah Milford?"

Ryan was interested now. "Yeah," he said. "Why?"

"I expect you know her family," Eli said.

Ryan shrugged. "A little. Her dad's a pastor."

"What's his name?"

"I don't know," Ryan answered. "Pastor Milford, that's all I know. She's got a brother, though. His name is Philip. He's a couple of years older than she is."

Eli nodded thoughtfully.

Ryan tried to study Eli's face but could read nothing there in the darkness. "Why?" he asked.

Eli gazed at Ryan for a few moments, until Ryan wondered if the old man had not heard his question. Finally he said, "Because I don't quite know everything."

A few more moments passed between them before Eli turned back toward the campsite. He patted Ryan's shoulder lightly and then left him sitting by the side of the stream in the dark.

the
thieves
.... ch. 5

SARAH AWOKE. The soft morning light filtered through the walls of her tent. But it wasn't the light that had awakened her. She smelled food.

Scrambling to her hands and knees, careful not to wake Alison and Liz, Sarah poked her head through the tent flap.

She couldn't believe the aroma wafting from the campfire, the most delicious smell she could imagine. Eli tended whatever was roasting over the fire. Jennifer and Jessica watched; their eyes looked as hungry as Sarah suddenly felt.

She looked around the campsite. There was no sign of activity in the boys' tent, and Duane was nowhere to be seen. She didn't want to face Jennifer and Jessica without reinforcements. She ducked back in the tent and let the flap close behind her.

"Alison," she called, patting her friend's foot. She grabbed Liz's toes in the other hand. "Liz, wake up."

Liz was the first to open her eyes and peek at Sarah. "What time is it?"

"I don't know," Sarah said, "but Eli's cooking something out there, and you won't believe how good it smells."

Alison sat up suddenly, as if an invisible puppeteer had yanked her string. "I smell it!" she said. "Let's eat!"

Sarah crawled out, with Alison right behind her. They were standing shoulder-to-shoulder by the fire by the time Liz crept out. They peered at the fire, wearing amazement on their faces as if they were performing a mime. A line of fish roasted on a thin metal spit over the fire, potato cakes fried in a banged-up skillet, and thin cakes of bread warmed on the rocks around the fire.

"Where did you get all this food?" Sarah asked.

"Did you catch those fish?" Jason asked.

Before Eli could answer, Duane, Jason, and Ryan crawled from their tents, adding their astonished gazes to the others'.

"Now," Eli said, "come and have some breakfast!" He carefully lifted the spit from the fire and held it out. One by one, his hungry customers retrieved their plates from their packs and held them out to Eli. He pulled a fish off the spit for each camper and then instructed them to help themselves to a potato cake and a piece of bread.

They ate heartily. Eli served himself last, and the sole subject of conversation during the meal was the meal itself.

"This is so good," Sarah said. "Thank you so much."

"I never expected to eat like this on the trail," Duane added.

"I still want to know," Jason insisted. "Where did all this food come from?"

Eli seemed to enjoy the question. He smiled at Jason and shrugged. "Out here," he said, "if you wake up early enough, the fish practically jump into your pan."

●■.●■.●■.●■.●

AFTER BREAKFAST and cleanup, Ryan joined the rest of the group around the fire circle for morning devotions. The day was early, and dew still clung to everything: trees, leaves, moss, tents, and the backpacks that had been hung from the branches around the campsite.

Jason again led the group in a period of singing, during which he repeated the songs they had sung last night, explaining that he was doing so for the benefit of their guests. After Liz led a brief time of prayer, Duane stood to address the group.

"Before we hit the trail this morning," Duane began, "I want to give us all something to think about and meditate on as we hike and talk together today.

"Last night, I said I wanted to explain something different about our relationship with God." The group nodded. "I mentioned last night how all of us have been separated from God relationally because of sin. And then I started to explain how God made his relational move. He sent his Son as a sacrifice so we could relationally connect to God. This relationship with God is different from any human relationship we have ever experienced. It is what gives us a real sense of belonging, of knowing we are accepted and loved in Christ. That connection allows us to live a life of happiness and meaning. But let me ask you a serious question." Duane paused for what seemed like an eternity. "Do you really believe all that?"

Ryan blinked at Duane. It seemed like an odd question. He looked slowly around the circle and saw that the others were slowly nodding their heads.

"Well," Duane continued, "what if I told you that none of the stuff I shared last night is true? What if I now claimed that everything God has said about the way to find a sense of belonging and love, the way to experience happiness and meaning in life is only imaginary—it doesn't exist in reality?"

"I would think you'd lost your mind," answered Jason. The others agreed.

"None of these things we claim that God does for us or provides for us is real if the Bible's claims about God and Christ aren't literally true. Not one of them—not salvation or happiness or meaning in life. If we can't count on all of it, then we can't count on any of it—which means we're back to square one in our quest for happiness and meaning in life."

"What are you trying to say?" Ryan asked. He felt thoroughly confused.

"As you hike today," responded Duane, "think about this: *There's no way God can be relationally real to you if the things you read about him in the Bible aren't literally true.* Think about that today and we'll discuss it more tonight."

⚓⚓⚓⚓⚓

DEVOTIONS ENDED and Sarah and the rest of the Westcastle team paused in the process of breaking camp to say good-bye to their overnight guests. Jessica waited while Eli hoisted her backpack in his hands and lifted it onto her back.

"Oh my," he said. "Guess I didn't notice last night how full your packs are. Are you sure you'll be all right with a pack that heavy? I'd be happy to shoulder your pack for a while."

"No!" Jennifer answered quickly. "No, that's all right. We'll be fine." She gripped her pack in both hands and, with a grunt, swung it onto her back. "It's not that heavy," she said. "Really."

Eli smiled indulgently and studied the weight on the two girls' backs. "They sure look heavy. But looks can be deceiving sometimes; they weren't too heavy for you last night, were they?"

"Shouldn't we be going?" Jennifer asked.

"We should," Eli answered. He turned to face the Westcastle group. "You all have been very kind. Thank you." His gaze landed on Sarah. "I hope this isn't the last time we see each other." He turned and looked expectantly at Jessica and Jennifer.

"Yeah," Jessica said. "Thanks."

Jennifer only nodded. "Right," she said.

Sarah felt herself relax as she watched the trio head back down the trail. She liked Eli, but it was sure good to see Jennifer and Jessica disappear around the bend in the trail.

Ryan was busy using Duane's camp spade to shovel one final scoop of dirt into the fire ring. He turned to see Sarah walking in his direction, only to trip over an exposed tree root and pitch to the ground.

He dropped the spade and hurried to her side. "Are you all right?" he asked.

Sarah grimaced and moved into a sitting position. She showed him the heels of her hands, which were covered with sand and soil; he brushed them off tenderly.

"No blood," he announced. When he looked at her face, she was watching him. He blushed.

"Thanks," she whispered, her eyes still studying him.

"No problem," he said. "Think you're all right?"

"Yeah," she said, shaking her head as though it had been all her fault. "It's these stupid shoestrings. They're way too long."

He watched her as she gripped one end of the wayward shoestring in each hand and prepared to tie it again. "Wait," he said. He reached to his belt, unsnapped the sheath to his camping knife, and pulled the knife out. "Want me to cut 'em?"

She smiled. "Wow," she said, staring at the knife. "You're like a boy scout."

He blushed again and dropped his gaze to the knife. "Is it too—"

"Dorky?" she interrupted. "No, not at all. That's not what I meant."

Immediately he wished he'd never brought the knife. "I was going to say, 'Is it too long on both shoes?'"

"Oh," she said, her voice tiny. "I'm sorry, I . . ."

Ryan shook his head. "It's okay." It wasn't, but he thought he should say it. He thought Sarah's remark revealed what she really thought of him. He wasn't surprised, just devastated.

"Here," she said, finally. She tied the errant shoestring and then extended both legs in front of her. She offered him a crooked smile. "Do what you have to do."

He managed to smile back. "I'll try not to draw blood," he said.

⬤▪⬤⬤▪⬤⬤▪⬤⬤▪⬤

BY 8:30 THAT MORNING, the Westcastle group was ready to hit the trail. Their bellies were full (thanks to Eli's hot breakfast), their water bottles were full, their tents were packed away, and their packs were securely strapped to their backs.

Before setting out, Duane showed them their destination and their route on the map, in case they got separated on the trail.

"Our lunch stop will be somewhere around Raven Point," Liz said. "If you're the first pair to reach it, take a break and wait for the rest of the team."

"But stay as close together as possible," Duane added. "We don't want to get too far strung out."

⬤▪⬤⬤▪⬤⬤▪⬤⬤▪⬤

"SO," JASON ASKED Ryan as the team set out two-by-two, "how far do you think they are?"

"Who?"

"Who else?" Jason answered. "Jennifer and Jessica. You think they're halfway there yet?"

Ryan shook his head. "Eli said it would take two hours just to get them back to their team. So they're not even halfway there yet."

"Good," Jason said.

Ryan looked at him curiously. "Why do you say that?"

"Think about it. If their team has to wait until ten o'clock this morning—after losing at least three or four hours, maybe more, looking for the girls yesterday—that should mean we've already got a six-hour jump on them. At least."

"I guess I hadn't thought of that," Ryan said.

"Well, now you have," Jason answered, brandishing his walking stick like a scepter, "thanks to the strategic thinking of—well, I'm too modest to say any more."

Ryan smiled. "You call that modesty?"

••••••••••

ALISON peeled the strands of a spider web from her face. "You should be glad I'm going first," she told Sarah. She gamely flailed her arms in front of her as though boxing with the spiders. "I hate these things."

Sarah stepped around Alison. "Remember, this is one reason Liz said to bring walking sticks." She thrashed the air in front of her with her stick, hoping to remove every vestige of spider webs still hanging across the trail, and then resumed the hike, leading the way for Alison.

"Can I ask you a question?" Alison asked.

"Sure," Sarah said.

"Did you understand what Duane was getting at this morning?"

"I think so," Sarah said. "Why?"

"I was thinking about Jennifer and Jessica."

Sarah's expression darkened immediately. "Why?"

"I kind of wanted to ask them what they thought."

Sarah climbed over a large moss-covered tree that

had fallen across the path. Once over it, she turned and offered a hand to Alison. "Why?"

Alison scrambled gracelessly over the tree and paused to brush the tree's moss and dirt from her clothing. "I don't think they're Christians, do you?"

"No," Sarah said flatly. "What's your point?"

"Maybe we should have talked to them about it," Alison said. "Maybe we missed a chance, you know?"

Sarah screwed her face up. All she wanted was to totally forget about Jennifer Brown, but nobody else on this trip would cooperate with that. She sighed deeply. "Whatever Jennifer and Jessica believe," she said, "is none of our business."

"It's not?"

Sarah shrugged. "I don't think so," she said.

"But I would think after hearing what Duane said about how God really wants to connect with us so we—"

Sarah interrupted. "You have to let people make their own choices, Alison." *Especially people who hate you*, she added silently, *and always make you feel about two inches tall.*

The two girls walked in silence along the trail. The light rustle of the wind in the trees and the occasional song of birds warning each other of the hikers' approach were the only sounds around them as they walked.

Finally, Alison broke the silence. "Can I *please* ask you another question?"

Sarah realized she had been frowning. She pivoted to face Alison, who was still behind her on the trail, and attempted a smile. "Have I ever been able to stop you?"

"Can't people still make their own choices," Alison asked, speaking slowly, as though the words were still forming themselves in her own mind, "after we witness to them?"

∎▪▪▪▪▪▪▪▪▪▪▪

"YOU'RE GOING TO kill me!" Ryan shouted.

Jason scrambled up a steep section of the trail like a third-grader climbing a jungle gym. Ryan watched him from behind, panting and sweating from exertion. They'd been on the trail almost four hours.

"Can't we just take a break?" Ryan pleaded.

"Breaks are for office workers and cubicle dwellers," Jason bellowed. "We are warriors!"

"*You're* a warrior," Ryan said. "I'm a wimp."

"No, don't say that!" Jason said. He extended a hand and helped Ryan up to the crest of the incline where he stood. "You're not a wimp. You're a mighty member of the soon-to-be winning SWAT team!"

Ryan shook his head. "Yeah," he admitted. He bent over and grabbed his knees to catch his breath. "And I'm a wimp."

Jason squinted at his companion. His voice took on a serious tone. "You're not serious . . . are you?"

Ryan didn't answer.

"Do you really think that?" Jason asked solemnly.

Ryan paused. He considered confiding in Jason. He thought he needed to tell somebody what he was going through, what he was feeling, what he had done back in Westcastle. But he was afraid what Jason would think. He was afraid that if Jason—anyone—knew what he was really like, it would ruin everything. Ryan was sure Jason would think he was crazy or pathetic—or worse.

Ryan inhaled deeply and straightened to face Jason. He smiled weakly and shook his head. "Nah," he said. "But can we at least take a break? I don't think I can make it to our lunch site."

Jason spread his arms and spun around as if he were showing off a castle. "You already have," he said. "Behold! Our lunch site!"

■ ▪ ● ■ ▪ ● ■ ▪ ● ■ ▪ ●

RYAN quickly shed his backpack and slumped to the ground in the shade. Leaning his back against a rock formation, he watched Jason take off his pack and guitar case and set them on the ground at his feet. "How long do you think it'll be until the others get here?" Ryan asked.

Jason pulled his water bottle from his pack and took a long drink. Then he shrugged and wiped his mouth with the back of his hand. "They're not far back. It could be any minute."

Jason returned the bottle to the side pocket of his pack and unzipped another pocket. Ryan watched while his hiking buddy searched that pocket and then started rummaging in another section of the pack without closing the first pouch. Jason continued his work, opening one compartment after another. Finally he straightened and stared at the pack as though expecting it to do something.

"Is something wrong?" Ryan asked.

Jason turned then and looked at Ryan. Then he turned back to stare at his backpack as he spoke. "I don't get it," he said.

"Get what?"

Jason scratched the back of his neck. "I can't find my food."

plotting
revenge
.... ch. 6

RYAN OPENED HIS MOUTH to speak again, but he was suddenly distracted by the sound of Duane, Liz, Sarah, and Alison arriving in the clearing together, chattering away like a convention of squirrels.

"Jason can't find his food," Ryan called out to the group.

"What do you mean?" Liz asked.

Jason shrugged, a look of bewilderment on his face. "I've searched my whole pack."

"You mean it's *all* gone?" Duane asked.

Jason nodded. "All of it," he answered. "I know I had it last night."

"That doesn't make sense," Duane said. "If animals had gotten to it, they would have made a mess."

"I know," Jason answered.

"My food's gone, too," Sarah said, peering into her backpack. "I know right where it was, and it's not there anymore."

Duane and Liz looked from Sarah to each other, and

then back to Jason. Within a few moments, they had all searched their backpacks.

"I don't understand," Liz said. "What could have happened to our food?"

"I understand," Sarah said. All eyes turned to her.

"What?" Ryan said.

"First she keeps me off the cheerleading squad," she said, "and now this!"

"What are you talking about?" Alison asked.

"Jennifer!" she said. "She stole our food! All of it!"

"Well, now," Duane said in a mollifying tone, "I don't—"

"No," Sarah insisted. "It was her. Don't you remember when Eli helped them with their packs this morning? He said he didn't remember them being that heavy last night!"

Alison's eyes widened. "You think—"

"They were so heavy because they had all our food!" Sarah said.

Duane, Liz, and Jason stared at Sarah as though they didn't want to believe her.

Alison shook her head slowly. "I'm so surprised," she said. "They seemed like such nice girls."

Ryan nodded and gazed at Sarah in apparent agreement. "They didn't seem to want Eli's help with their packs," he said. "You could be right."

"I *am* right," she said, her eyes glistening with tears. "You guys don't understand. Jennifer has done this kind of thing to me since third grade. She hates me."

"Oh, now, Sarah," Liz protested.

"It's true," Sarah quickly responded.

Jason slid over next to Duane. "You know," he said quietly, "Jennifer and Jessica did sleep by the fire last night. The rest of us were inside our tents all night."

Suddenly they were startled by a voice behind them. "Hello, on the trail!"

It was Eli's voice. He appeared in the clearing from a different direction than they had come from.

"Where did you come from?" Jason asked.

Eli smiled. "Oh, I managed to link them up with their party at Drover's Knob on Quail Ridge Trail. They were awful glad to see those girls, I'll tell you, but they'll have to push themselves mighty hard to make it to Nine Mile Crossing by nightfall. That's about the only place on Quail Ridge they could camp tonight, but even that'll take some doing."

"But," Jason asked, "how did you get here so quickly? We've been hiking all morning."

"Oh, I see what you mean," Eli answered. "Once I reunited those girls with their party, I was able to take a different path to get here. There's a nice little V-shaped Jeep trail that connects this here spot with my cabin." He held up two fingers to form a V. "You all are at the top left tip of that trail, my cabin's at the bottom point, and Nine Mile Crossing is the other tip. I cut across a short horse trail from where I left the girls to my cabin, and I'd no sooner walked in the door than I got a message to run a few things up to an observation tower up that direction." He pointed beyond them, the opposite direction from which he'd come. "And, lo and behold, I came across you folks again on my way there. Funny thing in the woods: You can go for weeks without seeing a soul, and then some days you seem to run into more people than in the middle of New York City."

Eli smiled. Jason smiled back and then turned his gaze to the rest of the team, who were looking on with awkward expressions. Eli looked from face to face.

"Is everything all right?" he said.

Everyone seemed to look at everyone else. No one seemed to want to answer, but eventually Duane explained that their food stores were missing. He didn't mention Jennifer and Jessica.

"I see," said Eli, his eyes wary.

Silence hung between them. Finally, Sarah broke the silence. "It was Jennifer and Jessica," she said. "They took our food. That should disqualify them."

"We can't prove anything," Ryan said. "Can we?"

Duane frowned. "I don't think it does us any good to think along those lines. We may have our suspicions, but like Ryan said, we don't really know anything for sure. The thing that puzzles me is, if they took our food out of our packs during the night, how did they know we wouldn't discover it when we went to fix breakfast?"

Eli's expression blanched. "I'm afraid I can explain that," he said. "I told them before I turned in that I planned to cook breakfast. I told them not to worry if they heard me up and around before everyone else."

Sarah looked at her teammates. "See?" she said, her eyes wide with anger.

The group seemed paralyzed. No one moved.

"What are we going to do?" Alison asked.

"We can't go two days without food," Ryan said.

"We could," Liz answered, "but it would slow us down. You really need carbohydrates on the trail."

"But this is supposed to be a wilderness *adventure*, right?" Jason suggested. "It's not supposed to be easy. Maybe we should look at this as a challenge. We've still got water, and we can eat plants and weeds and improvise all kinds of stuff." He whirled. "I mean, look at all the plants and stuff around us. I'm feeling hungry for a leafy green salad right about now!"

"Slow down, Daniel Boone," Eli said. "I wouldn't advise a tossed salad just yet. There are dangers in the woods. You can't just go picking leaves off plants and eating them. You wouldn't want a stomach full of poison ivy."

"I *know* what poison ivy looks like," Jason said.

Eli didn't reply immediately. While the others

watched, he glanced around for a moment, then he stepped aside and plucked a branch from a sprawling bush. He twirled the leaves between his fingers and showed it to Jason. "It's not just poison ivy you should be wary of," he said. "This here is elderberry. It's edible, and it has many different uses. You can eat the berries and the leaves, both. But if you do, you'll never make it to the summit you want to get to."

"You're kidding," Jason said. "Is it really that deadly?"

"No, not deadly," Eli answered. "You'll just spend more time crouching than you will hiking. It's an extremely effective laxative and purgative," he said with a smile.

"Does that mean what I think it means?" Alison asked.

Eli chuckled. "I think so," he said, tossing the plant to the ground near where he found it. "If you grind the leaves finely, mix it with water, and drink it, it'll clean you out real good, from the inside out. But if you used it that way without needing it, you would be in a desperate situation for the rest of the day." he said, adding that the leaves can also be rubbed on the skin as an insect repellent.

"Eli's right," Duane said. "We can't just go around eating things without knowing what we're eating. It's too dangerous."

"So . . . " Ryan ventured. "What are we supposed to do? Just turn around and go home? Let the other team win?"

"No way," Sarah vowed. "That's just what Jennifer would want."

"But we can't keep going without food," Liz said.

"I could give you what I have back at the cabin, but I'm afraid my cupboard's bare," Eli said. He hesitated just a moment before continuing. "But you could use my Jeep to get to town and replenish your stores." They all looked at him wordlessly. "It's at my cabin, just over an hour's hike down that trail and another hour or so into town. One of you could make that trip and be back in four or five hours. You could be back before dark."

Duane propped his hands on his hips. "That's very kind of you, Eli," he said.

Eli shrugged.

"But that would ruin everything!" Sarah protested. "We were winning until this happened!"

"Yes," Liz admitted, "but when we started this morning, we had a good half-day jump on Jennifer and Jessica's team. Now, we'll lose half a day ourselves—but we've got as good a chance as they do."

"That's why they did it, I bet," Alison said. "It wasn't just to be mean. They were trying to get their team back in the game."

"Yeah," Sarah agreed, "by stabbing us in the back!"

■ ▪ ▪ ■ ▪ ▪ ■ ▪ ▪ ■ ▪ ▪

JASON insisted on being the one to make the trip to town.

"I could go with you," Alison suggested.

Jason smiled but shook his head. "I can make better time alone." He winked at her. "Half the bathroom stops."

"Jason's right," Duane interjected. "He can handle the trip himself. The rest of us can make camp and rest up so we can make good time tomorrow."

Jason gave his guitar case to Duane and emptied his pack, making ample room for the groceries on the return trip. Just minutes after Eli offered his Jeep, the rest of the group watched Jason hike jauntily down the trail where Eli had appeared not long before.

Once Jason was out of sight, Eli spoke. "I'll be on my way, if you don't mind."

"Thank you," Duane said. "You've been very helpful . . . again."

Moments later, the five of them had the three tents off

their packs. Sarah watched Ryan as he unrolled his tent and began to clear a space for it, removing rocks and twigs from a flat section of the clearing. She turned to Alison. "Why don't you help Liz set up her tent?" she suggested. "I'll help you with our tent in a few minutes."

Alison agreed readily, and Sarah ambled over to Ryan's side. She tapped him on the elbow. He looked up at her in surprise, and she nodded toward the narrow path to the creek. Glancing back briefly at Liz and Alison, still absorbed in the work of preparing the camp, they walked a few steps down the trail toward the creek.

"Doesn't it bug you?" she said. "What Jennifer and Jessica did?"

He nodded vigorously. "Yeah," he said. "I think it stinks."

"With them stealing our food, they're going to catch up—they might even win!"

"I know," he said, shaking his head.

"What if I told you I have an idea?"

"An idea?"

"Yeah," she said. "Wouldn't it be great not to just have to sit here and take it?" *I've been doing that since third grade*, she added to herself.

He smiled. "Yeah, it would," he said.

"So you want to hear my idea?"

He nodded.

"What if," she suggested, "instead of hanging around camp doing nothing while we wait for Jason to get back, we find some reason to get out of camp."

"Okay," he said, his tone urging her to continue.

"Then we hike the trail Eli told us about," she continued. "We find Jennifer and Jessica's team and follow them until they stop for a break and take off their packs."

"Keep going," he said.

"This is the fun part."

As she spoke, Sarah's voice took on a conspiratorial

tone, and she leaned closer to Ryan. He'd never been this close to her face. He liked it.

"Remember that elderberry stuff Eli showed us?" Sarah asked.

"Yeah," Ryan said. His gaze was riveted to her face.

"We take some of that, as much as we can find, and grind it up. Remember, Eli said that if you grind it up and drink it, it'll—"

"Yeah, I remember," Ryan said, smiling.

Sarah's eyes sparkled. "We wait for our chance, and then when Jennifer and Jessica take off their packs, we sprinkle it in their water bottles and mix it up."

"Just their water bottles? Not everybody's?"

She shrugged. "Yeah," she answered. "If Jennifer and Jessica are—you know—the rest of the team will have to wait for them every time they have to stop. They might even have to wait for them to get better, which will give us the chance we need to get to the peak first."

Ryan smiled broadly. "That's pretty good," he said. His smile faded, however, as he thought of Mr. Robinson, the police officer who was a member of Jennifer and Jessica's team. "What if we get caught?"

"We won't," Sarah answered confidently. "But even if we do, what can happen? We can just tell them we got lost, just like Jennifer and Jessica did."

Ryan hesitated. Sarah had no reason to fear Mr. Robinson, but he did. He wanted to stay as far away from that guy as he could. But he didn't want Sarah to think he was afraid. And, he suddenly realized, he would be willing to do almost anything to spend more time alone with Sarah Milford. "Okay," he said finally. "Let's do it."

Suddenly, a voice sounded behind them.

"Hello, on the trail." It was Eli.

They both whirled to face Eli. He had come from the direction of the creek, and Ryan wondered how much he had heard.

"I was cooling my feet in the creek before finishing my trip," Eli said, with a slight nod in the direction of the creek. "I didn't mean to listen to your conversation. But I couldn't help but hear what you're planning."

Ryan exchanged a quick glance with Sarah. He felt suddenly guilty. This Eli seemed able to be everywhere, hear everything, and do anything: find lost hikers, fix a sumptuous breakfast, and ruin their plans for revenge.

"I don't often tell people what to do," Eli said. "But I do think it would be wise for you two to forget your plans."

"What are you going to do?" Sarah asked.

"Are you going to *tell* on us?" Ryan asked. He saw Sarah flash him a look; he thought it was a look of irritation, and he felt himself blush.

Eli paused before answering. "No," he said slowly. "But I think I will plan to drop in on the other team before they break camp in the morning. Now that I've learned of your plans, I'm just inclined to tell them to be absolutely sure they drink only *fresh* water . . . just to be safe."

Sarah and Ryan exchanged glances again. Eli was giving them a chance. No one would have to know about their plot.

"Okay," Sarah said. "You win."

Ryan nodded his agreement. "We'll go back to camp."

"Good," Eli answered.

"But we weren't gonna do anything those girls don't deserve, you know," Sarah said.

"Could be," Eli answered, smiling, as he prepared to pass them on the trail and resume his hike. "But it wasn't them I was most worried about."

truth and
reality
ch. 7

ALISON KNELT by the tent she and Sarah would share that night as Sarah and Ryan returned to camp together. She looked up from her work. "Where have you two been?" she asked.

Sarah shrugged. "Oh," she said, "nowhere."

Alison stood and propped her hands on her hips. "Are you still mad at Jennifer and Jessica?"

Sarah suddenly feared that Alison was somehow reading her mind. She shrugged and looked at the tent. "You set up the tent already?"

"All by myself." Alison smiled. "I wanted to surprise you."

Sarah threw her arms around Alison and hugged her. "You're so great," she said.

∎▪∎▪∎▪∎▪∎

SARAH sat beside Alison on a log facing the makeshift fire circle they had created in the center of the clearing where the paths converged. The five of them—Sarah, Alison, Ryan, Liz, and Duane—had finished setting up the camp-site a short while ago. Nothing remained to be done now but wait for Jason to return with food. "I can't believe we don't have any food," Sarah said. "They could have at least left us some crackers or jerky or *something*."

Alison shrugged. "Jason should be back in a few hours."

"Doesn't it make you mad?" Sarah asked. "That we have to sit here all day without food, while Jennifer and Jessica are laughing at us?"

Alison shrugged again. "I don't know," she said. "I try not to let things like that get to me."

Sarah stared at her. She didn't understand Alison, and she was sure Alison wouldn't understand how she felt. She waited a few minutes and then stood without a word, brushed off the seat of her shorts, and walked away. A glance at the tents revealed Liz, reclining half-in and half-out of her tent, reading a small paperback book, and Duane taking a nap. Ryan was nowhere to be seen.

Sarah found Ryan lying on a shaded outcropping of rock, dangling his feet in the rapidly flowing water of the stream. His eyes were closed. She studied him for a moment and then removed her socks and shoes and joined him on the rock ledge.

Ryan propped himself up on his elbows as soon as Sarah sat next to him. "Oh, hi," he said.

"Hi," she answered. She thrust her feet into the water and instantly withdrew them. "It's freezing!" she said.

He smiled. "It takes a minute, but you get used to it. It feels really good after a while."

"Before or after?" she asked.

"Before or after what?"

"Before or after your feet fall off from frostbite?"

He pulled his feet out of the water. "See?" he said. "Still attached."

Sarah dipped her feet in the water again and kept them there this time, though her eyes widened and her mouth formed a silent "O" while she adjusted to the mountain stream.

∎▪●∎▪●∎▪●∎▪●

RYAN watched Sarah, rapt with attention and admiration, until she finally leaned back on her elbows.

"I think I'm starting to like it," she said.

"Me, too," he answered.

She looked at him, and they locked gazes for a moment. He felt as though his admiration of her was written all over his face, and he blushed. "I–I've been thinking," he said.

"About what?" She seemed oblivious to his discomfort.

"I was just lying here," he explained, "not thinking about anything in particular, when I thought of another plan. It wasn't even like I had to think much, it just kind of popped into my head."

"What is it?" she asked. She lifted her feet out of the water and swung them, still dripping wet, across Ryan's legs, tenting them over his knees so she could face him directly. Her sparkling brown eyes reflected her intense interest in Ryan's plan.

He froze. She wasn't even touching him; her legs merely arched over his own. But he still had trouble concentrating. "We can still do it," he said, struggling to control his nervousness.

"How?"

He swallowed. "We could sneak out tonight."

"Tonight?" she said.

He nodded. "It's actually better that way. Eli said they'd be camping at Nine Mile Crossing tonight. This way we don't have to try to find them on the trail; we just go straight to their campsite. And we don't have to wait for them to stop and take a break, or anything like that. We just sneak into their camp, put that elderberry stuff in their water bottles, and sneak back out."

She peered at him with apparent fascination. Then her expression dimmed. "But what about Eli?" she asked. "Remember, he said he was going to make sure they all got fresh water in the morning."

"I thought of that, too," he said, his excitement building. "On our way back, we'll be passing Eli's cabin, right?"

"Yeah," she said, her tone urging him to continue.

"We can do something—let the air out of his tires, or something like that—so he can't get to the other team before they break camp in the morning."

"And then," Sarah interjected, gripping Ryan's arm with her hand, "we just sneak back to camp, and by the time everybody gets up in the morning, we're in our tents and nobody suspects anything."

He nodded. "We just have to make sure we're back before sunrise."

"Can we do that?" she asked.

"As long as nothing happens."

"What could happen?" she asked confidently.

❙ ❙.❙ ❙.❙ ❙❙.❙ ❙ ❙❙.❙

JASON arrived back at camp, tired but cheerful after a five-hour foray into town for supplies. He carried in his pack more than enough food to last for the rest of the trip. Soon after Jason removed his food-filled pack, the West-castle team sat around the fire circle, eating a rare meal of cold carryout chicken and corn on the cob that had been reheated over the campfire.

"I figured," Jason explained, "it would be a special treat to have some real food from the outside world. So I went through the drive-through!"

Duane grinned. "We're lucky you didn't eat it all before you got back here," he said.

"I would have had to kill you," Alison said, savoring the corn on the cob.

Jason shrugged. "But I would have died happy," he said.

∎▪▪▪∎▪▪∎▪▪∎▪▪∎

AFTER DINNER, the six team members divided the new food stores among themselves, bagged them into separate meals, and squirreled them away in their packs. By the time they were finished and their packs were safely hung from trees or stowed in tents, the light of day had dimmed, and night was approaching. Liz announced that it was time for devotions.

As Jason produced his trail guitar and led them in praise and worship, Sarah joined in as enthusiastically as anyone, closing her eyes and swaying slightly as they sang her favorite song, "Lord of My Life." When the singing concluded, Duane stood and faced the group.

"Okay," he began, "I said this morning that if the Bible's claims about Christ aren't true then the things we experience in God can't be real. What do you think?"

Alison spoke first. "That idea bothers me a little bit."

"Why?" Duane asked.

"Well," she continued, "I guess I've always thought that our faith made God real to each of us, not facts and stuff."

"All right," Duane said. "Maybe that's what faith does. It makes God real to us. What do the rest of you think?"

Ryan exchanged a shy glance with Sarah before speaking. "I think I agree with Alison. Whatever people believe makes it true for them. I don't think historical facts have much to do with it."

"Yeah," Sarah said. "It's like this: God is real to me because I believe in him. I think that's what believing does; it makes God personally real to you."

"Okay," Duane said. "Fair enough. But let me illustrate the implications of what you all are saying." He pulled something from his pack and began passing it around to the group. "I'd like each of you to take one of these."

"A grape?" Ryan said.

"Not just any grapes," Duane answered. "These are very special grapes and I would like each of you to eat one right now."

He waited in the crackling glow of the campfire while each of them popped a single grape into his or her mouth.

"Now, I know this is going to sound incredible," Duane began. "But the grape you just ate is a magical grape." He paused and scanned the faces of the group without smiling. "It is a magical grape that will give you incredible energy—so much energy, in fact, that you won't have to eat or drink another thing for a year. It's that nourishing."

Sarah looked around at the rest of the group. Their faces revealed nothing. "I'm so sure, Duane," she said.

"You don't believe me?" he said.

She rolled her eyes. "Don't be silly."

"Come on," he pleaded. "Why can't you believe me?"

"Because," Ryan jumped in, "there's no such thing as a yearlong energizing grape."

"Okay," Duane said. "No one has ever heard of these grapes before. But I'm telling you, just believe the grape you just ate will sustain you for a year—and it will."

"No, it won't," Alison said.

"Why not?" Duane asked, pressing the group for an answer.

"Because, like Ryan said, there's no such thing," she countered.

"So," Duane said, "you're saying if my claims about the grape aren't true, then its power isn't real. No amount of believing in the grape is going to make it work. If something isn't true, believing in it isn't going to make it real. Does that make sense?"

Sarah found herself nodding along with the rest of the group.

"Okay, then, let's take this to the next level," Duane said. "Let's say you all believe that you've sinned and are separated from God. Without a relationship with God you have no hope of happiness in this life and no hope of eternal life. But you believe Christ when he said he was God's Son, sent to die for you. You believe he is God's perfect sacrifice and that he will forgive you of your sins so you can have a real live relationship with him. Now, Sarah, let me ask you something," Duane said.

Sarah locked gazes with Duane as he continued.

"Did you trust in Christ as the perfect sacrifice for your sins? Has God forgiven you? Do you have a personal relationship with God?"

"Yeah, totally," Sarah responded, smiling broadly. "I prayed that prayer a long time ago."

"Okay. But what if Jesus was just a delusional man who claimed to be God's Son? What if he was a fraud? What if he never really performed miracles and didn't actually rise from the dead? What if he wasn't God's Son and the perfect sacrifice for your sins as he claimed? Then how could you know you're really forgiven? How could your relationship with God be real?"

Sarah's expression became serious. "You're starting to scare me," she said.

"I'm not trying to scare you," he answered, his gaze taking in the rest of the group. "What I'm trying to do is help you see that your prayers to God and belief in Christ aren't worth anything if the claims of Christ aren't actually true. If he isn't literally the true Son of the living God, then none of the relationship you think you have with God is real. If your faith is placed in a Christ who isn't who he claimed to be, then it's worthless."

"But doesn't my own experience of feeling forgiven by God count for anything?" Sarah asked.

"I know this shakes things up a little," Liz responded with a reassuring smile. "And Duane isn't trying to deny your relationship with God or cause you to doubt it. But that relationship is based not on what you *feel* is real, but on what is actually true about Christ. If Jesus isn't who he said he was, then he can't *be* what he said he'd *be* for you."

"But here's the great news," Jason interrupted. "The reverse is also true. If we can actually establish that Christ is who he claimed to be—the one and only, true Son of God—then we can know that your relationship with God is a total reality."

"And that's what I want to share with you tonight," Duane said. "I want us to dig deeper into these things."

■ ▫ ■ ▫ ▪ ■ ▫ ▪ ▫ ■ ▫ ■

AS DUANE reached for his pack again, Ryan leaned forward on the log where he sat between Jason and Alison. He was mildly surprised at the degree of interest he felt in what Duane was saying. He'd often thought that the things "church people" believed were in the same category as believing in life on other planets or the healing power of crystals: You just picked the belief that made you feel better, and for most people, the mere act of believing made it work. But Duane, Liz, and Jason were talking about Christian belief as if it were something entirely different. And Ryan found himself intensely interested.

Duane pulled out six sheets of paper. "I'd like each of us to read aloud something I've prepared here." He and Jason handed a sheet to each person in the circle.

"Each of the sheets has a number at the top," Duane continued. "I'll start, since I have number one. All this is written as if Jesus were saying it directly to us." Duane held the sheet of paper at an angle to catch the light from the campfire. He read:

> *I want you to be convinced that I am exactly
> who I say I am—that I am the Christ, the Son
> of the living God, and your only way to have
> a relationship with my Father. He and I are
> your only true source of life, happiness, and
> meaning. I want you not only to believe that I
> speak the truth; I want you to have a convic-
> tion that I am the truth. When you are
> equipped with such a conviction, you will be
> so convinced that I am the truth that you will
> act accordingly, no matter what the conse-
> quences may be. That is what convictions
> do—they give you the will to act upon your
> belief—and I will do the rest.*

Duane looked up from his sheet. "Who has number two?"

There was a slight pause, then Sarah answered. "I do." She began to read:

> *I want to have a real relationship with you—
> but on my terms, not yours. I know you want
> to be loved and accepted for who you are. You
> want to feel needed and valued. You want to
> belong. But you'll never experience those
> things in a relationship that relies on perform-
> ance. That's not at all the kind of relationship
> I offer to you. As my Word says, "Salvation is
> not a reward for the good things we have
> done, so none of us can boast about it"*
> *(Ephesians 2:9).*

When Sarah finished her reading, Duane scanned the others in the group. "Who has number three?" he asked.

Ryan began to read without further introduction:

> *It is true that you have done wrong—the*
> *whole human race is made up of nothing but*
> *sinners. It is true that, unlike you, my Father*
> *is infinitely righteous and holy, and he can't*
> *accept you the way you are. To have a rela-*
> *tionship with him you need to be like him, so*
> *you need to change. But you can't. If you've*
> *ever tried, you know that you can't act like*
> *him, you can't conform to his image, you*
> *can't even approach his holiness. But you*
> *don't have to. As my Word says, "Don't copy*
> *the behavior and customs of this world, but let*
> *God transform you into a new person by*
> *changing the way you think" (Romans 12:2).*

Ryan finished reading, and Duane asked for sheet number four to be read. Alison inhaled deeply and spoke with a quiver in her voice:

> *I know you want to do right. You want to*
> *please. You want to be a good person. But all*
> *your trying doesn't work. It's just not in you.*
> *All your efforts to reform your behavior still*
> *don't get you what you long for. You can say,*
> *just as Paul said, "I love God's law with all*
> *my heart. But there is another law at work*
> *within me that is at war with my mind. This*
> *law wins the fight and makes me a slave to the*
> *sin that is still within me" (Romans 7:22-23).*

Ryan was aware, as Alison finished reading, that a quiet but strong emotion had settled on the group. Everyone seemed to be listening and responding to the words on the page as if they had been scrawled there by the very hand of Jesus. His gaze traveled around the circle and finally settled on Jason, who was the next to read:

> *My Father's condition for a relationship with*
> *you isn't based on you performing, conform-*
> *ing, or reforming. No, because of me—and*
> *what I have done for you—he draws you into*
> *a relationship based solely on transforming.*
> *But it's not something you have to do; it's the*
> *result of His transforming power working*
> *in you.*
>
> *As I inspired Paul to write, I "died for*
> *everyone so that those who receive [my] new*
> *life will no longer live to please themselves. . . .*
> *What this means is that those who become*
> *Christians become new persons. They are not*
> *the same anymore, for the old life is gone. A*
> *new life has begun!" (2 Corinthians 5:15, 17).*

No one spoke when Jason finished. Instinctively, all eyes went to Liz, the only person in the circle who hadn't yet read. Liz said:

> *I'm talking about a real transformation, in*
> *which I give you a new nature so you can live*
> *differently. Peter stated accurately that my*
> *"divine power gives [you] everything [you]*
> *need to live a godly life" so "that you will*
> *escape the decadence all around you caused by*
> *evil desires and that you will share in [my]*
> *divine nature" (2 Peter 1:3-4). In this trans-*
> *forming relationship, my Father adopts you*
> *into His family and invites you to call him*
> *Abba, which means "Daddy." You become one*
> *with us, so you can start enjoying all the*
> *happiness and meaning I desire for you.*
>
> *This isn't something you can create for*
> *yourself. But it can become a living reality in*
> *you when you become convinced that I am*

who I say I am—the Son of God—and are transformed so that you can enjoy a thriving family relationship with my Father.

"great flying monkeys!"

cried Ratsbane, clapping his rubbery frog hands against his great head in a gesture of pain and despair. "This cannot be happening." His obsidian eyes glared at the video image of the Westcastle group. He spun and faced the classroom of demons.

"Why?" asked Stench. "What's the big deal?"

"Big deal? I'll tell you the big deal, you festering mound of meat. If those Westcastle kids respond to what that Cunningham slime is teaching them, they will experience the mighty transforming power of the Holy One—and then there will be heaven to pay!"

Boos and hisses punctuated Ratsbane's warning.

"But it's far from over," he said. "Furblight!"

She grimaced at the sound of her name.

Ratsbane continued with an air of urgent command. "What were you doing while that Duane character was talking?"

"I–I was trying to keep Sarah's mind focused on her plans to get even with Jessica." She gulped loudly, as if afraid to continue. "I wanted to keep her distracted, so the truth will stay in her head and not have a chance to get to her heart."

Ratsbane clapped his hands together once more in a gesture of approval. "Furblight has just earned herself a session in the worm tank!"

Disappointed moans and groans, like those of first-graders whose recess has been canceled, bounced off the slimy rock walls of the room.

"What are you talking about?" Stench protested. "What's this 'keeping it in her head and not in her heart' mumbo jumbo?"

Ratsbane turned and glared at Stench. "You still don't get it, do you, Stench? An amateur tempter and tormentor—like you—has no chance of succeeding down here. Furblight is performing a textbook strategy of how to handle damaging truth. Once truth enters a human head, the task of hell is to just keep it there, where it will do no harm. What must not be allowed is to let the impact of that truth touch their heart. Let them hear truth, even accept it if they must . . . but at all costs keep it intellectual." He let out a cackling, wicked laugh that reverberated off the walls of the cold, stone room.

"That's why Furblight's method was perfect. She didn't try to induce disagreement in young Sarah Milford's mind; oh, no, she was much to smart for that! It would have been much harder if the girl's heart had been engaged. She worked hard at not letting Sarah feel the impact of that truth experientially.

"All of you must learn from Furblight. Whatever you do, keep them from the responding to the truth. Keep their hearts dull to the meaning of the truth. Keep them from responding to the Enemy's unconditional love and acceptance. Keep them from experiencing the transforming power of the Enemy's love. Keep them from tasting the happiness and meaning that is found in a right relationship with him." He turned from addressing the group and focused his glazed eye on Furblight.

"Go ahead, Furblight," he said. "Keep it up." He reached a slimy hand toward her and, in a gesture that startled and horrified every demon in the room, gently stroked the top of her furry badger head.

the
evidence
.... ch. 8

SARAH SUDDENLY felt a chill run up her spine. She stood suddenly and walked quickly over to her pack and pulled out a jacket. When she turned around, she saw that everyone in the group was watching her.

"Sorry," she said, slipping the jacket on and tiptoeing back to her spot by the fire. "I felt a chill."

Duane seemed unperturbed. "Do you understand," he continued, "why Christ wants you to be thoroughly convinced that he really is the Son of God? Do you see why Jesus' statement in John 14:6, when he said, 'I am the way, the truth and the life, no one can come to the Father except through me,' is so important?"

"I think I'm seeing it now," Alison said. "It sounds pretty exclusive, but he's saying it that way because there's no other way to have a relationship with God."

"You're exactly right," Liz said. "And all the conditions we put into relationships—performing, conforming, and . . . what's the other one?"

"Reforming," Jason added.

"Right," Liz continued. "None of those conditional relationships will provide us with the happiness and meaning that God's transforming relationship brings."

"But, remember," Duane interjected, "there is no transforming relationship with God if Christ isn't the one and only Son of God."

"So the question is this: How can we know beyond a reasonable doubt that this man called Jesus is who he said he is, the Christ, the Son of the God, who took on human form to save us and restore us to right relationships with the Father?"

"And you're saying we can't just believe that?" Sarah asked.

"Sure you can," Liz answered. "But blind faith doesn't give you the assurance that what you feel you have is actually real. God wants you to have an intelligent faith, not blind faith. He wants you to have a rock-solid belief that he is true and real. And the way to do that is to look at the evidence."

"Now that doesn't mean," interrupted Duane, "that examining the truth about Christ eliminates the need for faith. No amount of evidence can create a one-hundred-percent certainty. But like someone said, intelligent faith is trusting in what we have reason to believe is true. It's then that our believing in Christ can become a conviction. And convictions are what he wants. He wants us to be convinced that he can and will do everything he promised to do in our lives."

"Right," Liz said. "So if Christ is really the Son of the one true God, the only hope for the human race, as he claims to be—there ought to be some proof or evidence that his claim is true. And there is.

"One category of evidence is found in all the predictions the Jewish prophets made about how the Messiah would come and what he would be like. You see, more than four hundred years before Christ was born, God had his prophets foretell a lot of very specific things about the Messiah. Each and every one of those things the prophets predicted had to be fulfilled by the Messiah. It's like the directions we have to reach Shiloh Peak. If we follow the directions, step by step, we should get to the top.

"Those prophecies about the Messiah were so numerous and specific that if they were all fulfilled in one person, we could be sure he was the true Messiah, God in the flesh, the Son of God and Savior of the world."

Jason rose from his seat and passed out small slips of paper to everyone in the circle. "We'd like you all to take turns reading again. What you will be reading are some of the specific prophecies that gave the ancient Jews the information to help them recognize and identify the true Son of God, the Messiah."

Liz looked at Ryan, who sat on one end of the short semicircle of people around the fire. "Ryan, why don't you go first?"

Ryan read from the small slip of paper in his hands, a reference to Genesis 22:18, which predicted that the Messiah would be among the descendants of Abraham. Then he read the fulfillment of that prophecy, from Matthew 1:1, the record of Jesus' birth.

Liz nodded and looked next to Sarah.

Sarah read next, citing Micah's prophecy about the Messiah being born in Bethlehem. Alison followed, reading the promise of a virgin birth. Duane went next, and a few moments later, everyone in the circle had read an Old Testament prophecy and the account of its fulfillment in the life of Jesus.

After everyone had read, Liz said, "What you've just heard are a mere eight prophecies that predicted the Jewish Messiah and Savior of the world. Every one of those prophecies was fulfilled in one person, Jesus, who was born over two thousand years ago. But do you know how amazing that is that those prophecies were fulfilled in one person? And do you know what that means?"

◼ ▪ ◼ ▪ ◼ ▪ ◼ ▪ ◼ ▪ ◼

(the inside story)
beyond a reasonable doubt

HUNDREDS OF YEARS before Jesus' birth, Jewish prophets spoke and wrote many prophecies about the Messiah. Those prophecies were intended to put people "on the alert," to help them recognize the Christ, the Son of the living God, when he came. They can do the same thing for us today.

For example, look at just eight prophecies given through the ages about the expected Jewish Messiah:

1. that he would be born in Bethlehem (Micah 5:2);
2. that he would be born to a virgin (Isaiah 7:14);
3. that a forerunner would announce his arrival, a "voice in the wilderness" (Isaiah 40:3);
4. that he would ride victoriously into Jerusalem on a young donkey (Zechariah 9:9);
5. that he would be betrayed by a friend (Psalm 41:9, Zechariah 11:12);
6. that he would be crucified (his hands and feet would be pierced), but his bones left unbroken (Psalm 22:16; 34:20);

7. that he would die (be "cut off") 483
   years after the declaration to rebuild
   the temple in 444 B.C. (Daniel 9:24-26);
   and

8. that he would rise from the dead
   (Psalm 16:10).

All of those prophecies, of course, were fulfilled in
Jesus' life, death, and resurrection. But do all those
fulfilled prophecies really establish Jesus' identity as the
Messiah, or could they have happened by coincidence?

For the answer to that question, we need only turn to
the science of statistics and probabilities. Professor Peter
W. Stoner, in an analysis that was carefully reviewed and
pronounced to be sound by the American Scientific Affili-
ation, states that the probability of just *eight* prophecies
being fulfilled in one person is 1 in 10^{17} (that's 1 in
100,000,000,000,000,000).

Look at it this way: If you were to take
100,000,000,000,000,000 silver dollars and spread them
across the state of Texas, they would not only cover the
entire state, they would form a pile of coins two feet deep!
Now, take one more silver dollar, mark it with a big red X,
toss it into that pile, and stir the whole pile thoroughly.

Then, blindfold yourself, and starting at El Paso on
the western border of the state, walk the length and
breadth of that enormous state, from Amarillo in the
panhandle to Laredo on the Rio Grande all the way to
Galveston on the Gulf of Mexico, stooping just once along
the way to pick up a single silver dollar out of that two-
foot-deep pile . . . then take off your blindfold and look at
the silver dollar in your hand. What are the chances that
you would pick the marked coin out of a pile of silver
dollars the size of the Lone Star State? *The same chance that
one person could have fulfilled just eight messianic prophecies in*

one lifetime.

And that's just the beginning! There are over three hundred messianic prophecies in the Old Testament that were fulfilled in *one person,* Jesus Christ—all of which were made more than four hundred years prior to his birth. In other words, it is nearly unthinkable to imagine that the Old Testament prophecies about the Messiah could have come true in one man unless, of course, he *is*—as he himself claimed—"the Messiah, the Son of the Blessed God" (Mark 14:61), the One who was and is and is to come (see Revelation 4:8).

That means that there is an overwhelming amount of evidence to prompt us to believe, with an intelligent faith, that Jesus Christ is truly the Son of the one true God. That makes a relationship with God—the source of all happiness and meaning in life—a real experience. In other words, because of what is true about Christ, a transformed relationship with God is a real possibility. But because it is a real possibility doesn't necessarily make it real to every person's life.

As the enemy knows, just because we believe in our heads that Jesus is who he claimed to be and that a relationship with God is real doesn't mean we will magically find happiness and meaning in our lives. Something else is needed to get that truth from our heads to the emotional, relational heart of our lives. Because if that doesn't happen, our relational transformation isn't complete.

into the darkness

ch. 5

THE WESTCASTLE CAMP was quiet. All were in their tents after devotions.

Ryan lay on his back, carefully monitoring Jason's breathing, waiting for some sure sign that his tentmate was asleep. As he waited, he thought about what Duane had said as they sat around the fire circle for devotions. As he thought back on his life—especially the last few weeks—he could see more clearly what he'd been searching for.

I was stupid to let Adam and Seth talk me into doing all that stuff, he told himself. *I didn't care about the electronics stuff or anything else. I just wanted someone to like me, to think I was okay.* He glanced at Jason. *But it was crazy to think I could get someone to like me by going along with them and just getting into trouble. What I really want is somebody to care about me for who I really am.* Tonight—maybe for the first time in his life—he began to think that such a thing might be possible.

He smiled and nodded slowly. He was glad he came

on this trip. It had been good for him. Though now he realized he was about to do something dangerous. *It'll be worth it, though, because I'll be doing it with Sarah Milford. I can't let her down.*

He rolled in his sleeping bag until he faced Jason. He was inches from Jason's ear.

"Jason," he whispered. "You awake?" He waited. He heard nothing but the almost imperceptible sound of Jason's rhythmic breathing.

Ryan carefully stole out of his tent. Once out, he squatted at the entrance, turned, and slowly zipped up the screen door of the tent behind him. His eyes scanned the campsite; he watched Duane and Liz's tent for a few moments and then peered at Alison and Sarah's tent. There was no sign or sound of movement anywhere.

Ryan was sitting on a log by the fire circle when Sarah finally emerged from her tent. He didn't know how much time had passed, but it had been long enough that he had begun to worry that she might have fallen asleep.

"Are you ready?" she asked when she approached.

He nodded. Her eyes seemed to sparkle even in the trifling light of the night. "Let's go," he said, standing. "Do you have a light?"

She waved a flashlight in front of his face without turning it on.

"Mine's still in my pack," he said. "I'll get it."

They padded quietly out of camp and down the trail Eli had appeared from many hours earlier. It was a wider trail than most, with twin ruts just wide enough for a Jeep to traverse. The forest canopied over their heads, blocking out most of the light from the half-moon and stars. When they had walked for about five minutes, Ryan announced that it was probably safe to turn on their flashlights. They did so.

"Are you scared?" Sarah asked.

He shook his head and lied. "No. You?"

"A little," she said. "Things sure look . . . different . . . at night."

"Yeah," he said.

"I sure hope we can find our way back. We don't even have a map."

"You heard Eli; it's just 'a V-shaped Jeep trail.' Our campsite is at one end of the V, his cabin's at the bottom, and their campsite is at the other end of the V."

"The hardest part," Sarah suggested, "will probably be finding the other arm of the V once we get to Eli's cabin."

"Yeah," he agreed. They walked in silence for a few moments, until he asked, "Did you bring the elmerberry, or whatever it is?"

"Elderberry," she corrected. "I've got it right here." She patted her pocket.

He could hear the smile in her voice. "It'll be enough, right?" he asked.

"I don't know," she answered. "Eli didn't say how much, but I'm not too worried about that. He made it sound like it doesn't take a whole lot."

"Yeah, you're right." The forest seemed to get darker as they walked, though "darker" hardly seemed possible. They could barely see anything beyond the beam of their flashlights, and those they kept trained on the trail just in front of their feet.

"What do we do if Jennifer and Jessica pulled their packs in their tent?" Sarah asked.

"Well," Ryan said. He gripped a low-hanging branch and held it back, allowing Sarah to pass before letting go. *"Someone's* pack is going to be hung from a tree. We'll just mix the elmerberry into every water bottle in every pack we see; it'll slow the whole group down no matter whose water we spike."

She giggled. "You keep calling it elmerberry," she said.

"Sorry," he said.

"No," she answered. "It's cute."

The comment warmed him somewhere inside. The skin on his arms erupted with goose pimples. He wanted desperately to keep the conversation going, but it was Sarah who spoke next.

"I really hope we can get Jennifer and Jessica," she said. "It won't be as much fun if it's not them."

• ▪ • ▪ • ▪ • ▪ • ▪ •

SARAH AND RYAN were tired and clammy when they reached Nine Mile Crossing, but they easily located the other team's camp. They stood for a few moments on the edge of the clearing. The night air had become heavy as they hiked, and the wind had increased. The wind buffeted the trees overhead, turning the quiet night into a howling, unruly cacophony, but no one seemed to stir.

They quickly spied several packs hanging from low tree branches. Working together, they removed the water bottle from each pack, poured in some of the ground elderberry leaves, recapped it, and shook it vigorously before returning it to its place. The water bottle in the third pack was nearly empty; after a moment's hesitation, Ryan shook his head and returned the bottle to the pack without adding any elderberry.

Too risky, he mouthed.

Sarah understood. It would be too easy for their trick to be discovered in such a small amount of water.

They progressed to the next pack. Sarah recognized it. She tapped Ryan on the shoulder and pointed to the pack in an exaggerated motion. She nodded. *Jennifer*, she mouthed.

Ryan carefully doctored the water bottle in Jennifer's pack as Sarah opened several pockets in the pack. She pulled out a couple of clear bags of food and showed them to Ryan, her eyes wide and her lips tight. The bags held her food. She moved to put one of the bags into her pocket.

Ryan stopped her. He placed his lips against her ear and whispered. "If she notices it's gone, it might make her suspicious."

She hesitated, but only for a moment. Nodding solemnly, she pulled the bag from her pocket and returned it to Jennifer's backpack, carefully zipping up the pocket and moving on.

They saw one more pack hanging from a nearby tree, a sufficient distance from the closest tent for them to feel somewhat safe. They treated the bottle of water from that pack. Then, after they exchanged satisfied nods with each other, Ryan led the way out of the camp.

●■●■●■●■●■●

A FULL FIFTEEN minutes after they left the other team's camp behind, Sarah clamped a hand on Ryan's shoulder from behind and turned him around to face her.

"We did it!" she squealed.

He smiled and nodded. "Yeah, we did," he said.

She suddenly threw her arms around him and hugged him. He froze.

"Thank you," she said. "I really appreciate your doing this with me." She released her grip, and he realized—too late—that he hadn't even hugged her back. It had all happened too fast, and he had been too surprised to know how to respond. He wished he could get the moment back; he couldn't believe he hadn't wrapped his arms around her, and he mentally kicked himself for squandering such a golden opportunity.

"Oh, you know," he stammered. "No problem."

She whirled and started walking again, leaving him to follow, trying to regain his mental balance while she chattered excitedly about what would happen when Jennifer and Jessica got up in the morning, expecting to race for Shiloh Peak, only to have to take frequent—and inconvenient—breaks along the way.

"Okay," Sarah said still excited about their accomplishment. "What did we say we'd do to keep Eli from warning them?"

"I think we were going to disable his Jeep," Ryan responded. "We could flatten the tires or something."

"Good idea," Sarah remarked. "That should keep him from reaching their camp before they head out."

With their plot finalized they trudged forward. Their energy was flagging as they reached Eli's cabin clearing again, more than three hours after they had left their own camp. Since they had left Nine Mile Crossing, the weather had become increasingly angry. Wind whipped the trees and even their flashlights seemed to dim in the glowering, imposing darkness of the night.

Eli's Jeep rested at one corner of his cabin.

"It's pretty close," Ryan said, as they paused to catch their breath and stared at the dark cabin and the shadowy form of the Jeep. "It's right by that corner of the cabin. What if he hears us?"

"It'll just take a few minutes," she said.

He nodded grimly. "No lights," he said, waving his flashlight between them.

She nodded back.

They crossed the clearing in a trot. As they crouched together beside the Jeep, the wind swirled in the clearing and tossed up dirt and dust, prompting them to close their eyes and shield their faces with their arms. Sarah set her flashlight onto the ground and felt around the rim of the tire for the air valve.

"I can't find it," she said, raising her voice to compete with the howling wind.

Suddenly, a light blazed on in one of the cabin windows.

"He heard you," Ryan shouted in panic. "He's coming!" He gripped her arm to pull her away to safety.

"No!" she shouted back. "Wait!" She reached for his belt, unsnapped the sheath to his camping knife, and pulled the knife out.

"What are you doing?" he said.

She gripped the knife in both hands and thrust it into the sidewall of the front tire, flattening it immediately.

They heard the unmistakable sound of a door banging open as she plunged the knife into the back tire, before the two of them dashed away into the violent, stormy darkness without risking a look behind them.

* * *

SARAH RAN through the dark with Ryan's knife in her right hand, mindless of the danger she held in her hand, oblivious to the risk of falling, desiring only to put as much distance as possible between themselves and the cabin behind them. The glowering sky enclosed them, and the path that had seemed so broad earlier that night seemed to constrict like a snake around them. The darkness seemed to press in on them, closing in, as if any second it might touch them.

They ran until Sarah cried, "Stop!" She grabbed her knees and stooped to catch her breath, still gripping the knife. A light flashed on, and the beam came back to where she stooped. When she looked up, she saw that Ryan was panting, too.

She extended the knife toward him, careful to point the blade away from his body. "Your knife," she said, between gasps.

She felt him gently pry it from her fingers. "You're not—" he said, panting, "you're not supposed to run with knives."

He returned the knife to its sheath on his belt. "Where's your flashlight?" he said.

"Back there," she said. "Somewhere. I might have dropped it when I grabbed your knife."

A blade of lightning suddenly split the sky, and Sarah jumped and gripped Ryan's arm with both hands. A dry wave of thunder rolled angrily over them, and the savage winds buffeted them.

"We'd better hurry," Sarah said.

"Yeah," Ryan agreed. "Here." He held his flashlight in front of her. "You take this."

She shook her head. "No. I'll just stick close to you," she vowed. Her voice quivered. "Let's just go."

∎▫◦∎▫◦∎▫◦∎▫◦

ANY OTHER TIME, Ryan would have enjoyed a night-time hike with Sarah Milford pressing against him, hanging tightly on his arm. But he began to question his ability to get Sarah back to the campsite. The storm intensified with every step; the forest whipped and wailed around them like a flailing blinded giant. Dust and leaves swirled wildly. Branches and limbs crashed to the forest floor, sometimes narrowly missing them. Their progress slowed, and they bowed their heads against the wind.

Large drops of rain began to pelt them, bullying their way through the churning canopy of trees overhead. Suddenly Sarah slipped, nearly pulling Ryan down on top of her.

"Are you all right?" he shouted over the din of the storm. He helped her to her feet and shone the flashlight up and down her form.

"Ryan," she cried, "I'm scared."

Cold blades of fear stabbed his own heart. "I know," he said. "But we're going to be fine." He wished he believed it.

Thunder crashed suddenly in their ears, and Sarah released her grip on Ryan's arm. He spun and reached out to grab her, but she tumbled away from him with a pain-filled scream.

"Sarah!" he called. She had been right beside him a

moment earlier, but she was gone now. She had just disappeared into the darkness. He pointed the meager beam of his flashlight here and there, but saw nothing except a pattern of thick darkness and threatening movement. He called again, but the wind seemed to blow his cries back into his mouth.

trapped

ch. 10

SARAH SHOOK all over. Swaying and slipping, she had
let go of Ryan in an attempt to steady herself. She had lost
her footing and slipped down a precipice of some kind,
and she had landed with a jolt on a narrow ledge. She
struggled to stand and eventually found her feet under
her. She leaned against the rocky hillside, unable to see
much of anything around her and afraid to take a step in
any direction.

For a moment, she thought she had gone blind. The
wind roared around her and the storm lashed at her
cheeks, but the darkness was complete.

"Ryan!" she called, in a voice charged with panic.
"Ryan, I'm here. Can you hear me?"

She waited and heard nothing. She stuck a foot out
into the darkness before her, but could feel nothing solid
beneath where she poked her toes. For all she knew, the
mountainside fell away in front of her and if she stepped,
she would fall away, too—how far she could fall, there was

no way to know.

"Ryan!" she called again. "I can't move!"

She listened again, and thought she heard something. A faint cry. The wind seemed to be rolling up the hill and blowing the cry farther away from her.

She screamed then, a loud, sustained cry of desperation. And then she saw a light.

She looked up. A dim circle of light shone above, perhaps ten feet over her head. She called to it.

"Ryan, is that you?"

Another crack of lightning lit the sky, followed instantly by a crash of thunder, and then the rain descended. It drove against the hillside in cold, biting, nearly horizontal torrents. Sarah tried to wrestle her raging emotions under control and peered around her; the flash of lightning had lit what seemed to her to be a thin ledge of rock interrupting an otherwise sheer drop into the vast darkness.

But she heard Ryan's voice then. He had found her. He pointed the light at her, and then turned it under his chin to light his face as he called to her.

"Are you hurt?" he cried.

"No," she answered quickly. She hesitated. She hadn't considered the possibility until Ryan suggested it. She performed a quick inventory of her limbs, a swift search for pain. "I don't think so," she said. She gazed up through the slashing raindrops. She estimated his distance as eight or nine feet above her.

"What happened?" Ryan called to her through the storm.

She ignored his question. She wasn't sure she knew. She just knew that she had slipped away from him and landed here. "Shine your light down here," she said. "I need to see where I am."

The light of his flashlight was weak, at best, but it revealed more of the hillside than she could see without it.

"Over there," she said, pointing.

Ryan obeyed, and scanned the hillside with the light. They both saw the marks of her descent through the brush. The trail had been washed out by the rain, creating a precipitous mudslide from the trail to the ledge where she stood now. The hillside in front of her seemed impossibly vertical. Above her, just below the small circle of light, jutted a craggy outcropping.

"I'm coming down!" he said.

"No!" she screamed, her panic swelling. She shouted through frightened coughs. "You'll hurt yourself!"

"Hold on," he insisted.

"No! Ryan, listen," she said. "I don't know how I got here, but if you try to come down, we might both be stuck!" She tried to shield the rain from streaming down her face.

"I've got to do something!" he said. She heard the panic in his voice, and it frightened her even more.

"Here," she said. "Shine the light over here." She pointed behind her. "Maybe there's a way out behind me."

He obeyed, but the light from the flashlight barely stretched the distance to where she pointed. Sarah took only a few steps before the tiny ledge ended in a rock wall; she dropped to her knees, looking for the signs of a trail or some way around or over the outcropping above her head and back to the trail where Ryan waited.

"What do you see?" he asked.

Sarah wiped the rain from her forehead with the heel of her hand and tried to stem the growing panic in her heart. "Nothing," she answered. "I think I'm trapped."

"Just sit tight, then," Ryan commanded. "I'll find a way down."

"Ryan, no!" she cried. "Please don't. If you come down here, we'll never get out!"

"Sarah—"

"Do you think you can make it back to camp and get

a rope or something?" she asked.

"I'm *not* leaving you here!"

"We can't stay here arguing all night," she reasoned. "Do you think you can do it in a half hour?"

There was no answer. She lifted her gaze to make sure the light was still there. It was.

"Yeah, maybe," he said, finally. "But I can't just leave you here."

"You have to, Ryan," she persisted. "You have to get a rope. That might be the only way to get me out of here."

Again there was no immediate answer. The wind and rain whipped the hillside as if intent on punishing the mountain for resisting.

"I could bring back help," he answered.

Sarah was torn momentarily, but her fear quickly vetoed any concern for keeping their midnight mission a secret. "Yeah," she agreed. "Just get going."

"I could leave you the flashlight," he said.

"No! You need it to find your way to camp and back here. If you get lost . . . "

"Okay. Are you sure you'll be all right?"

"Ryan Ortiz, if you don't leave right this minute, I'll never forgive you!"

The light turned her direction. "I'll be back, Sarah. Don't worry, okay? I promise."

She watched the light move again and then it was gone. She was alone.

Ryan had been gone for a while; Sarah had no hint of how much time had passed, but she feared it had only been a few minutes. She was wet, cold, and frightened. The rock overhang afforded some shelter from the wind and rain, but she was afraid to move around in the darkness, afraid she might lose her footing and tumble farther down the mountain.

She heard a strange sound; it wasn't thunder. It was a low rumbling, intermittent, not far off. She puzzled over it for a few moments. Then she realized what it was, and the realization made the hair on the back of her neck stood up.

It was a low, throaty growl.

❖❖❖❖❖❖❖

RYAN'S courage flagged. He was afraid not only that his flashlight batteries would die before he made it to camp but also that he might slip in the ever-increasing muddiness of the forest path and injure himself.

The storm raged unabated, and the rain had transformed the Jeep trail into a small but surging stream that slowed him down and made running difficult and dangerous. He was soaked and tired. His shoes weighed three or four times their normal weight and his legs grew leaden.

Suddenly, his progress was arrested in midstride; a soggy spot in the trail had gripped his right foot. With a ferocious grunt, he dragged his leg out of the mud, leaving his shoe behind.

"No!" he cried. He turned, shining the flashlight into the flowing water. He tucked the light under his arm and straddled the deepest part of the stream, aiming the flashlight's beam where he had last stepped. His shoe had disappeared. He groped in the water and mud while the rain pelted his back.

He knew he still had a long way to go, and the rain, mud, and darkness were slowing his progress as it was. To make the rest of his journey back to camp in bare feet would make matters worse, especially if he injured himself by stepping on a rock or twig.

Finally, his fingers felt something distinctly unlike rock or mud or water. He gripped it with both hands, and yanked his shoe from the stream with such force he nearly pitched himself backward when the shoe came free.

Lurching to the side of the trail, he leaned against a gnarled tree trunk and, after much fumbling, wrestled his shoe back onto his foot, tying it as tightly as his trembling fingers allowed. Brushing his dripping hair back out of his eyes, Ryan carefully resumed his journey, zigzagging back and forth across the trail, avoiding the deepest parts of the stream the storm had created.

SARAH froze with fright. The cold rain pelted her mercilessly, but she was oblivious to every drop. She knew only that something—something big—was in the darkness nearby. She lay still and held her breath, trying to breathe as shallowly as possible. She listened carefully for another sound of its approach.

So intently did she listen that it took her a few moments to realize that she had been smelling the animal for some time. A wild, musky smell seemed to surround her. She snapped her mouth shut in a panic, realizing that if she could smell the animal . . . it could certainly smell her.

Then she heard it again, behind and above her: a low rumble like an engine. She twisted carefully and gazed upward. She saw two tiny white glints of the animal's eyes, peering back at her, and she wanted to scream and close her eyes, but she felt frozen in place, hypnotized by fear.

Oh, God, her heart cried out. She was helpless, and she knew it. Trapped as she was, she was at the animal's mercy, easy prey. Suddenly her tongue came unstuck. "Please, God, no," she said.

Suddenly, she heard a noise that sounded like a gunshot, and a huge weight crashed through the leaves and trees above her and rushed down the hillside toward her. She screamed and covered her head with her arms. She felt and heard and smelled the creature all at once, and it seemed to brush past her with humanlike shouts and groans. She continued to scream, and the animal seemed to scream back at her, until suddenly she realized that it was no longer above her, nor even on top of her, but somewhere below her on the hillside. She stopped screaming.

For a moment, all she could hear was the sound of her own frantic breathing and the wild beating of her heart. Then a voice: "Are you hurt?"

She felt disoriented. It was a human voice. She blinked against the rain, as if clearing her vision would clear her confusion. Then she realized the voice had asked a question.

"No," she answered, her voice tiny and trembling in the midst of the storm.

"Good," the voice said.

Eli?

She heard clawing and scrambling in the brush of that hillside, and the sound carried closer, little by little, until a dark form appeared nearby and pulled itself onto the ledge where she sat hugging her knees against her body. After another moment, he was there beside her, clutching a muddy rifle in his hands.

"Are you sure you're not hurt?" he asked, panting from the exertion.

"You're bleeding!" she said. She touched his face and quickly pulled her hand back. Blood streamed from his scalp.

He nodded. "I won't know how bad it is until I can get some light. Do you have a lantern?"

She shook her head, remembering where she left her flashlight. She paused, then asked, "What happened?"

"A mountain lion," he answered. "I smelled it and heard it before I saw it. I had just planned to avoid it, but then I heard you."

"It–it was going to attack me?"

"Afraid so. It must have been pretty hungry; they tend to steer clear of humans unless they're trapped."

"I'm the one who's trapped," she said, her voice still quivering. "I slid down here and couldn't figure out how to get back to the trail."

"That might explain it. He must have thought you were wounded."

"Can you get us out of here?" she asked.

"Let's see," he said. He set the rifle down against the rock face under the overhang and crawled around the ledge, never more than a few feet from where she sat.

"There has to be a way out," she said.

He probed the area some more, then returned to her side and squatted next to her. "I'm sure there is," he said. "But there's not much use in trying to find it in all this rain and darkness."

"So what are we going to do?"

"The smart thing," he said.

"What's that?"

"Nearly anything except scrambling around in the dark and the mud. That's a recipe for disaster."

"Ryan went to get help," she said. "When they come, they should be bringing back a rope or something." *If he can remember where I am.*

"Good," Eli said. "Let's see what I can do about a fire."

She saw him grimace as he crouched and scoured the sheltered space for twigs and brush. "You really are hurt, aren't you?" she asked.

He had quickly assembled a small pile of kindling, and pulled a small slab of flint from his pocket. "It hurts like a wildfire," he said. "If I can get a fire going under this ledge, I can get a look at it."

"I'm so sorry," Sarah said. She vowed never to forgive herself if anything happened to Eli, and then she remembered that not long ago, she had slashed this man's tires. If he were seriously hurt, there would be no way to get him quickly to a medical facility. He repeatedly struck his flint with a rock and then leaned his lips into the pile of sticks, blowing gently, stopping, then blowing again, until a flame flickered and leaped to life. When the tiny fire burned confidently, he scouted the area and assembled a collection of the driest articles he could find. "That ought to do us for a while," he said.

In the flickering light of the fire, Sarah saw the glistening wetness of the blood in his hair and on his face. When she offered to help, Eli shook his head but accepted her help in removing his shirt and inspecting the row of long, gaping gashes that reached from his shoulder blade, under his arm, and across his belly.

"He got me good," Eli said with a groan. He instructed Sarah how to rip his shirt into bandages, and showed her where and how to tie them in order to stem the bleeding. When she finished, he thanked her.

Sarah's eyes filled with tears. "You shouldn't thank me," she said.

He gingerly placed another stick on the fire. "Sure, I should," he said. "I feel better already."

"No," she insisted. She paused, and Eli waited. She shifted in the small space, crossed her legs in front of her, and began twisting one of her muddy shoestrings around her index finger. "Ryan and I, we . . ." She stopped, gathered herself, then started over. "I was at your cabin earlier tonight. I–I slit the tires on your Jeep." She braced herself.

"I know," Eli said. He gazed directly at her. His eyes were kind, gracious.

Sarah flashed him a momentary look of surprise. "Oh," she said at last, feeling as if understanding was slowly seeping into her soggy brain. "That's why you followed us. Because I slashed your tires."

"No," he said.

"No?"

He shook his head.

"Well, then . . . why?" she asked.

He still fixed her with his gaze. "To make sure you were safe."

She studied him. The blood from his head wound still streamed down the side of his face. "Why?" she asked. "Why would you go to such trouble for people you barely know?"

"Well, Princess," he said, "that's not completely true."

She stared. "What did you call me?" she said.

"I suppose I should explain," Eli said.

"What's going on?" she asked. None of this was making any sense to her. This man who had saved her life—who had wrestled a mountain lion for her—was a stranger to her, yet he had called her "Princess," a name only her parents called her.

"Your name is Sarah Milford. You live at 228 Lake Street in Westcastle. Your parents' names are James and Marjorie. How am I doing?"

Sarah stared at him. The sounds of the storm swirled around her, and the warmth of the fire had already begun to fill the small space on the hillside, but she felt as if she were in a dream, and none of this was real.

"You see," Eli said, "I knew you before you were born. And I've loved you ever since."

"But how—"

"I'm your grandfather."

SARAH SAT SPEECHLESS in the flickering light of the tiny fire. She felt as though the spiraling tendrils of smoke from the fire were wrapping themselves around her brain, making it impossible to grasp what Eli was saying. "I don't understand," she said.

"Your parents have told you that you're adopted," Eli said. It wasn't a question. He spoke the words as if he already knew the answer.

"Yes," she said.

"But you've never known your biological family." Again, it was a statement, not a question.

"No," she said. "My parents wanted me to wait until this year."

Eli seemed to be weighing his next words, but it was Sarah who spoke next.

"They said I could make contact with my birth family right after this youth group trip."

Eli nodded. "I know," he said. "They contacted me

about a month ago. We actually made plans for me to come to your house next week. But I never imagined I'd meet you up here."

"Me either." They both fell silent. The storm swirled around them, and the wind came and went unpredictably. But the tiny fire flickered bravely. She lifted her gaze and peered carefully at Eli. "I think it would be okay with my parents if . . . if you told me about my birth family."

"What is it that you do know?" Eli asked.

She shrugged. "Some things. That my birth mother loved me and that's why she gave me up for adoption. They told me she died when I was about two years old. And I've always gotten birthday gifts from my grandfather." She stopped. She remembered that the gifts from her grandfather were often addressed to "Princess Sarah," or simply, "Princess." She'd never considered it strange, because her father had always called her that, too.

"Your mother, Elizabeth," Eli said, "was my daughter. Priscilla, my wife—your grandmother—died of a stroke ten years ago."

Sarah drew up her knees and wrapped her arms around them as Eli continued talking.

"Elizabeth was very young when she had you. She was just out of high school. And still in college. Giving you to your new family was the hardest thing she ever did in her whole life."

"In her whole life," Sarah repeated. She gazed at the fire and spoke without looking up. "How did she die, exactly?"

"She was on her way home from college," he said, his eyes misting. "It was Christmas break, and she had been doing so well in school. Her car hit an icy patch of road . . . "

The old man and the girl fell into silence. The music of the fire, the raindrops smacking into leaves and the increasingly distant rumble of thunder over the hills provided a percussion accompaniment to their thoughts.

Finally, Eli broke the spell of silence.

"I never stopped loving you," he said. "You've been constantly in my heart since before you were born. For sixteen years, I've wanted to connect with you. I've longed for a way for you to know me, for you to know how much I love you, how very important you are to me."

"Why didn't you do anything?" She turned her head only slightly and watched for his reaction out of the corner of her eye.

He frowned and started to speak, but paused. "Sarah," he said, "I guess you know your adoption was a closed adoption."

She shook her head without looking at him.

He nodded. "Your parents, the Milfords, had the responsibility to decide if and when and how to tell you about your adoption and your biological family. And they decided that it was best to wait. This is the time they have decided we can contact each other."

"Did you ever try?"

He stirred the fire slowly and added to it before speaking. "I've written you a letter every year just before December nineteenth."

She looked at him. "My birthday."

He nodded. "Sometimes I go on for many pages. There's so much I've wanted to tell you." His voice quivered and his speech thickened with emotion. "But we've been separated all these years, and it's been hard on me. I can't tell you how many times I've wanted to see you and sweep you up in my arms and say the things a grandfather wants to say to his granddaughter."

"Where are they?" she asked. "The letters, I mean. Did you send them all?"

He nodded. "Yes, but always with the knowledge that your parents would decide which ones were best for you to see and at what time. But that didn't stop me from writing. Those letters have been waiting for you all this time,

for you to read, for you to find out that you have a grandfather who wants you and loves you, no matter what, no
matter how long he has to wait."

"My parents told me they have some things that
they'll let me look through when I get back. But do you
think all of them got through?"

"I think so," he answered. "But I also made a copy of
each letter for myself. I copied every one, every word, by
hand and have saved them all these years. I wanted to do
everything I could to make it possible for you—someday,
somehow—to know me . . . and the love I feel for you."

A single tear escaped Sarah's eye and ran down her
cheek. She made no effort to wipe it away. "I can't believe
it," she said.

"Oh, I hope you can," he said. "I hope you can do
more than believe it. I want you to *know* it."

She turned her head and looked at him. Her lip quivered into an ironic half-smile. "I can't believe I slit my own
grandpa's tires. Can you forgive me for that?"

He smiled. "Can I forgive you? You're more than
forgiven."

She wrinkled her forehead. "More than forgiven?"
she asked. "What do you mean?"

Eli smiled warmly. "If you were anyone else, I'd just
have to forgive you. But because of who you are, I more
than forgive you. You're my lost granddaughter whom
I've always loved but never known up close and personal.
You could have burned my cabin down, and I'd still love
you."

"But you don't know what I'm really like," Sarah
responded.

"Oh, I *do* know what you're like—more than you
think—because you're the daughter of my very own child.
Your parents chose to love you. They graciously took you
into their home and made you their much-loved child.
And they've been wonderful parents. But you see, Sarah,

you were already my grandchild by birth, and I loved you since before you were born. My love isn't based on what you do; it's based on who you are—my very own flesh-and-blood granddaughter. Nothing you do or don't do will ever change that. And my, how I love you."

"Oh," Sarah murmured. "I love you, too, Grandpa." She unfolded her arms and reached for him, and they embraced each other tightly.

※ ◦ ● ● ◦ ● ● ◦ ● ● ◦ ●

RYAN WORRIED that he, Duane, and Jason wouldn't be able to find the spot where Sarah had fallen from the trail. But it was easier than he thought.

The rain had finally subsided by the time they returned to the washed-out part of the Jeep trail, and with the three lights they carried, it was much easier to see what had caused Sarah's fall. Softened and muddied by the rain, the hillside had given way, probably at the precise moment that Sarah and Ryan had arrived at that point in the trail. Because Ryan had been a couple of paces ahead of Sarah, he had remained on the trail while Sarah had been swept down to the ledge below.

"Sarah!" Ryan called, even more frantic when he saw the extent of the damage to the trail. He turned to the others. "This is where she fell!"

They all called Sarah's name and paused.

"Down here," Sarah responded.

Ryan pointed his light to the edge of the hill and nodded to Duane and Jason. He unshouldered the looped rope that he had insisted on carrying from camp and handed one end to Jason.

"I smell smoke," Duane said. "Do you smell smoke?"

Ryan waited until Jason had anchored the rope to a sturdy tree and then quickly looped the rope around his waist and again around his upper arm and backed toward the hillside. A moment later, he stood on the narrow ledge and gaped, slack-jawed, in surprise.

He scanned the scene in silence: the small fire, and a wet, but comfortable, duo: Sarah . . . and Eli. Sarah smiled at him. He could see, in the light of his flashlight, that she had been crying. He adjusted the beam and saw that Eli, too, had apparently shed tears.

"Boy," she said. "Have we got a lot to tell you."

"we must stop this!" screamed Ratsbane. "What just happened on that hillside should *never* be allowed to happen! I should have known," he said, pacing back and forth, talking now more to himself than to the others. "I should have seen it coming. I've seen so many of the Enemy's tricks that I should have smelled this one a mile away!"

He swiveled and pointed a warty frog finger at the elevated video screen. "Curse you!" he shouted, his ant mouth spitting venom as though he were a snake. His clawlike mandibles worked back and forth in agitation. Slowly, he regained composure and turned again to address the class.

"My worthless, hopeless inferiors," he said. "Let me explain. I'm afraid that Furblight's human subject—the girl named Sarah—has just *experienced* the kind of unconditional love and acceptance she has been told about these last two days."

"Whoop-de-do," Stench said, twirling a crusty finger in the air. "It's just her grandfather. Big deal, right?"

Ratsbane glared at him. "You fool, do you understand

nothing? The danger of her experiencing unconditional love and acceptance—from her grandfather or anyone—is that it so vividly resembles and reflects the Enemy's love and acceptance."

Stench's finger froze in the sulfurous air of the cavern. "Oh," he whispered.

"And if her experience of unconditional love and acceptance opens a doorway in her heart to the Enemy's love and acceptance, she might just . . ." A visible shudder wracked Ratsbane's toady body. "She might just take the next step of conviction."

"What step is that?" asked Furblight.

A foul croak emerged from Ratsbane's throat. "It is the step of relying upon the Enemy to transform her into one mighty loving, soul-winning human powerhouse that can shake the walls of hell," he bellowed. "And we can't let that *happen!*"

**the trans-
formation**

ch. 12

SARAH HAD never been so happy to see Liz and Alison.

She entered camp with Eli, Duane, Jason, and Ryan and was immediately greeted by her crying friends, who were visibly relieved to see her safe and sound. A fire blazed in the fire ring, and Sarah ducked into her tent to change into dry clothes. Duane fetched a towel and change of clothes for Eli while Liz doctored his wounds and made him promise to see a doctor in the morning.

Soon, though no one gave explicit instructions, everyone came together at the fire ring, tacitly acknowledging that sleep would be impossible and some sort of gathering was in order.

It began slowly and sheepishly but, with gathering momentum, Sarah and Ryan told the story of their night mission. When Ryan finished telling about Sarah's fall, and his journey to camp to get help, Sarah took over, dramatically relating the story of Eli's encounter with the mountain lion.

"How did you know to bring a rifle?" Jason asked Eli.

"I don't leave the cabin at night without a rifle," he answered.

"Were you scared?" Alison asked.

"Terrified," Eli answered immediately. "I would never willingly tussle with a mountain lion, but in this case, I had to. I couldn't take the chance that something might happen to Sarah."

"What made you follow us in the first place?" Ryan asked.

Eli exchanged a knowing glance with Sarah, and she took over the narrative once more. She related in detail what she and Eli had talked about, and what Eli had revealed to her about their relationship.

"No way!" Alison breathed, when Sarah repeated Eli's revelation that he was her grandfather.

Sarah smiled and continued. Her voice quivered and her hands shook as she told them about the letters Eli had written. She proceeded to repeat virtually every detail, nearly word for word, of what Eli had said to her on that hillside. When she finished, no one spoke. They stared, shook their heads, or wiped tears from their eyes.

■ ▫ ● ■ ▫ ● ■ ▫ ● ■ ▫ ●

After a long silence, Duane spoke from where he sat. "I'm always amazed at how God works," he said. He poked at the fire with a long stick. "But this is one of the most amazing things I've ever been a part of."

Several people nodded as though they understood what Duane meant.

"I mean, it's incredible enough to learn that our new friend Eli is actually Sarah's biological grandfather . . ."

"I didn't even know you were adopted," Alison said.

"Yeah," she said. "I've known since I was little."

"But," Duane continued, "I'm especially awed by the fact that God chose this week—this wilderness adventure—not only to reveal Eli and Sarah's relationship, but to use it to illustrate the exact stuff we've been teaching and talking about since we started this adventure."

Sarah turned a quizzical look on Duane. "What do you mean?"

"Remember what Eli told you on that hillside?" Duane said. "He said—correct me if I get it wrong—but he said something like, 'I love you not because of what you do or don't do. I love you for *who you are.* You're a member of my family. You're a part of me. You're my granddaughter. And nothing you do or don't do will ever change that.'"

Sarah exchanged glances with Eli and then nodded at Duane. "That's almost exactly what he said."

Duane smiled broadly. "Don't you see? That's what God says to you." He turned and scanned the faces around the campfire. "We are his lost, estranged children who are no longer alive in him. And he is our waiting, loving Father, who desires to give us life—a re-birth. And he went to great lengths to say to us, 'Sarah . . . Alison . . . Jason . . . Liz . . . Ryan . . . Eli—I love and accept you not because of what you do or how you look or how you talk or anything like that. And because of the sacrifice of my Son I will transform you into a living member of my family, a part of me. And nothing you can ever do will change my love for you and my acceptance of you.'"

Sarah's eyes burned with interest and excitement. Her mouth hung open as she began to understand. "Oh," she said. "Oh . . . "

"Not only that," Duane continued, "but just as Eli has been writing Sarah for all these years, putting his thoughts and feelings on paper, in the hope that someday she might come to know him—and his love and acceptance— through the things he's written, so has God. Your heavenly Father has written about his passion for relationship with you, saving up his words for thousands of years, just so you can know him and deepen your relationship with him—and he with you."

He closed his eyes and lowered his head for a few moments, while every gaze around the circle was trained on him. Sarah sat close enough to see his lip quiver, a sight that prompted her own eyes to fill with tears. He seemed to struggle for composure for a few moments and then lifted his gaze again. "When Eli left the warmth and safety of his own cabin to search for Sarah, he did so knowing that she had lashed out at him. He knew who had slashed his tires." He glanced at Eli, who nodded his agreement. "But he wasn't deterred in the least by the damage she had caused. He chose to search for her in the darkness and the storm, because he knew the danger . . . and he also knew who she was.

"So he went to find her, and he did—even putting his own life on the line to save her. And when he won the contest and defeated the enemy, he revealed his heart to her and told her not only who he was but also who she was—and how long and desperately he had wanted her to know him and his love for her.

"That," Duane said, "is the story of God in Christ, who came seeking every one of us and put his life on the line. He won the contest and defeated the enemy . . . so that we might have a transforming relationship with him."

$$\bullet\bullet\bullet\bullet\bullet\bullet\bullet\bullet\bullet\bullet\bullet\bullet$$

(the inside story)
the four "r's" of a transformed relationship

SARAH, RYAN AND ALISON have been struggling to figure out what brings true happiness and meaning to their lives. Yet all three of them have been trying to create that in their own way—mostly by attempting to live up to someone else's or their own expectations. They have viewed all their relationships through a distorted lens that requires that they perform, conform, or reform in order to feel like they are loved, accepted, needed, wanted and valued for who they are.

But now they are coming face to face with a new way of understanding and experiencing relationships—the four *R's* of a transforming relationship with God:

> **R**ecognize you have a problem with God.
> **R**ealize that God is the solution to your problem.
> **R**espond to the Truth with conviction.
> **R**ely upon God to live in and through you.

Recognize Your Problem with God

Most of us recognize that we have done wrong in our lives. The Bible says, "For all have sinned; all fall short of God's glorious standard" (Romans 3:23). But few of us recognize that our problem is really with God. We think we should have the right to decide what is best for our lives. When we think and live that way we disregard God, the only true source of happiness and meaning in life. "No one has real understanding," the Bible says; "no one is seeking God. All have turned away from God; all have gone wrong" (Romans 3:11-12).

Recognizing your problem with God means you acknowledge that you have turned away from God and don't have enough understanding in life to decide for yourself what is right. God's Word says it like it is. You "were once so far away from God. You were his enemies, separated from him by your evil thoughts and actions" (Colossians 1:21).

Realize That God Is Your Solution

The next step toward a transforming relationship with God is to realize that you can't help yourself; God alone is your solution. "When people sin," the Bible says, "they earn what sin pays—death" (Romans 6:23, NCV). Your problem with God has earned you death—separation from God. And you are totally incapable of solving that problem.

Sixty-four percent of kids just like you believe that Christ came to earth to teach you how to live better so you can go to heaven. But living better doesn't cut it with God. You can't earn a relationship with him by trying to perform good deeds or conforming to the expectations of others or trying to reform your sinful life. Because of your sins, you're dead, and dead people can't pick themselves up, dust themselves off, and bring themselves back to life! Dead is—well, dead.

You see, Jesus didn't come to earth to make bad people good; he came to earth to make dead people live. "The Spirit of God, who raised Jesus from the dead, lives in you. And just as he raised Christ from the dead, he will give life to your mortal body by this same Spirit living within you" (Romans 8:11). That is your solution, found only in the work of God in Christ.

Respond to the Truth with Convictions

Once you recognize that you have a problem with God and realize that he alone is the solution to your problem, the next step is to respond to the Truth—the Person of Truth, Jesus Himself—with convictions. A truly transforming relationship with God involves agreeing with Jesus, who said:

> *I am the way, the truth, and the life. No one*
> *can come to the Father except through me.*
> *(John 14:6)*

*You will die in your sins; for unless you
believe that I am who I say I am, you will die
in your sins. (John 8:24)*

*I am the resurrection and the life. Those who
believe in me, even though they die like everyone else, will live again. They are given eternal life for believing in me and will never
perish. Do you believe this? (John 11:25-26)*

Do you really believe this? Are you convinced that
Jesus Christ is who he said he was: the resurrection and
the life, the only way to salvation, the only solution to your
situation? When you respond to Christ—the Truth—with
a conviction that he is your one and only solution, he is
ready to transform you from death to life, from separation
from him to a new, thriving, fulfilling, meaningful relationship with him. "To all who believed him and accepted
him, he gave the right to become children of God. They are
reborn! This is not a physical birth resulting from human
passion or plan—this rebirth comes from God" (John 1:12-13).

Rely on God to Live in and through You

Believing with convictions in Christ as your salvation
provides the will to turn away from sin and your belief
that you have the right to choose your own way, and turn
to Christ to transform you into a child of God in relationship with him.

The Bible says, "God sent [Christ] to buy freedom for
us who were slaves to the law, so that he could adopt us as
his very own children" (Galatians 4:5).

Our response to Christ—believing in him with
convictions, turning from our sin, and turning to him—
also includes a trust and reliance on him to live the transformed life in and through us. Like Paul said, "I have been

crucified with Christ. I myself no longer live, but Christ lives in me. So I live my life in this earthly body by trusting in the Son of God, who loved me and gave himself for me" (Galatians 2:19-20).

The young man or woman who takes these crucial steps will experience true happiness and meaning, because those things come only from the unconditional love and acceptance that can be ours in Jesus Christ. In that relationship—and only there—we will go beyond relationships that are built on performing, conforming, or reforming and will instead experience the transforming power of a right relationship with God . . . which, in turn, can transform all other relationships in our lives.

■ ▪ • ▪ ■ • ▪ ■ • ▪ • ■

SARAH stood suddenly. Her face was streaked with tears, and she struggled to control the emotions that rose up from within her. Even through the haze of her tears, she saw that every eye turned on her and that everyone in the circle was willing to wait until she could control her emotions and find her voice.

"I–I just have to tell you all," she said, haltingly. "I can't sit here anymore without admitting that . . . that, even though I've been raised in a Christian family and I've been a Christian for a while now, I haven't been the kind of Christian I ought to be—not really. I mean, I–I've known all along who God is, but I haven't really been convinced he can be to me what he wants to be. I've acted like God is whoever I say he is and that I can pick and choose what I think is best for me, but I know that's not true now. My life has been consumed with trying to get love and acceptance and all I've gotten is resentment and anger toward some people . . . and I know that breaks God's heart." With those words, her emotions rose again, and she took a moment to regain control. "I want to confess my resentment and unforgiveness of others and the fact that I've been trying to go my own way. I guess I just want you all to know how sorry I am and how much . . . how much I want to start over."

Sarah buried her face in her hands then, and she felt rather than heard the others get up from their seats around the fire and encircle her. They prayed, first Liz, then Jason, and Duane . . . and finally Eli. When she lifted her head and looked around the circle, she saw that there wasn't a single dry eye among them.

Suddenly, however, Sarah noticed that Ryan was no longer part of the group standing around her, though she felt certain he had been there at the beginning. He sat on the log by the fire, by himself, his arms propped on his knees and his face buried in his arms. His arched back rose and fell irregularly. He was sobbing.

"everybody grab one!"

Ratsbane croaked, his voice edgy with panic. He upended the box he had just carried into the cavern classroom and dumped it onto the table at the front.

"What are these?" clucked Rankmeat, the turkey-headed demon with the body of a cow. With great difficulty, he picked up one of the strange devices with his two front hooves.

"We have very little time," Ratsbane explained. "As of now, you are no longer students; you are tempters and tormentors. And these are your Palm PETs," he said, referring to the sophisticated handheld Prime-Evil Transducer devices, the latest technology of hell which allowed demons to tempt and torment their human targets with little more trouble than it takes to program a VCR. It was new technology, still in the experimental stages, and Ratsbane had to overpower three demon drudges in order to steal them. But he knew it would be worth it if it meant stemming the latest Westcastle rebellion. His demon soul had been singed far too many times by Duane and Liz Cunningham and the exasperating kids in their youth group.

"But we're not ready!" Stench whined, his odiferous breath repelling even the hell-hardened demons around him.

"You've got that right," Ratsbane said. "You're the sorriest bunch of underdemons I've ever known. But I have no choice. The walls are already starting to crumble. Feel that quaking under your feet?"

Several demons looked at the floor, realizing for the first time that a rumbling had started beneath them. Ratsbane snatched a remote control from the desk and pointed it at the video monitor in the corner. "We have to work quickly to bring things back under our control."

The screen flickered and flashed momentarily, and finally the scene around the fire circle appeared. Several demons quickly covered their eyes or buried their heads in reaction to the disturbing sights and sounds. The sounds of choking, gurgling, and gnashing of teeth began to build in the room.

"Rankmeat!" Ratsbane yelled. "Get to TechCentral right now and tell them I have a DefCon 4 situation onscreen; tell them I want a live GreenFeed *now!* And I don't want to hear any excuses. Got it?"

Rankmeat saluted clumsily and disappeared through the classroom door. Ratsbane whirled and faced the roomful of trembling demons.

"This isn't supposed to happen," he said, his twitching antennae betraying his nervousness. He pointed to the screen, which depicted the group from Westcastle around the fire ring. "This isn't supposed to happen. This was supposed to be a Kum Ba Ya songfest around the fire. But this has gotten out of hand.

"But," he said, gritting his teeth and straightening his frog spine, "a true demon of hell must recognize when things turn sour and call in the appropriate firepower. In this case, the first step is a GreenFeed."

At that moment, as if on cue, Rankmeat lumbered back into the room with a bulky device in his hands. He set it on the desk, opened it like a laptop computer, and adjusted the thin triangle of wire that protruded from the back like an antenna.

"This," Ratsbane explained, "is a GreenFeed."

The demons gathered around and peered at the large screen, which seemed to be focused on the very same scene as the video monitor in the corner, except this screen shone with a luminous green tint. Ratsbane pointed a Palm PET at the GreenFeed and the scene rotated slowly.

"We must determine first what hellish resources exist on location." He continued pointing the Palm PET and poking several of the buttons on the control. "There!" he said. He aimed at the screen. "Do you see them?"

"I see them!" announced Stench. "In the trees! Two winged demons, in the trees!"

Ratsbane nodded seriously. His mandibles began to twitch, and his antennae crossed and uncrossed. "In the trees! Do you know *why* they're in the trees?"

The room fell silent. No one dared to venture a guess.

Ratsbane aimed the Palm PET and rotated the view again until it focused on the Westcastle group. Almost in unison, the demons gasped in horror. Aided by green-screen technology, the visual feed revealed Sarah, Ryan, and the rest of the group . . . encircled by a contingent of radiant white angels, their flaming swords upraised, their lips moving in unison as they sang their prayers for the humans they guarded.

A fracture suddenly appeared in Ratsbane's skull, and it seemed to his students that he might explode. He turned his glassy eyes on them and let out a string of demonic curses that caused even their hardened hearts to quake. "That," he spat, "is what happens when you let your human subjects *pray!*"

■ ■ ● ■ ● ● ● ■ ● ● ● ■ ●

JASON camped beside Ryan on the log by the fire and draped an arm across his tentmate's shoulders. He waited, and they all watched, as Ryan sobbed quietly. Several times, Jason asked a question, but so far Ryan could respond only with a nod, a shrug, or a shake of the head.

Long moments passed by, and finally, Liz placed a hand on Ryan's shoulder and began to pray aloud, asking God to calm Ryan's emotions and help him to express himself. A few moments later, Ryan inhaled deeply, like a swimmer who's just crested the surface of the water after a deep dive.

Slowly, then, little by little, Jason succeeded in drawing out the feelings that Ryan couldn't express. Ryan confessed that he'd never before understood—or even really believed—that God could care about him, much less adopt him into his family and transform his life. He explained that, as Sarah had described what had happened between her and Eli that night, he had sat by the fire wishing that something like that could happen for him.

"And then," he said, still panting slightly and wiping the tears from his face, "and then Duane said that it did happen for me."

"That's right," Jason said. "It did."

Ryan looked up hopefully at Duane. "I mean, that's what you were saying, right?" he asked. "That God wants a relationship with me and because of Christ I can be transformed into God's child?"

Duane smiled and nodded. "Right," he said.

"But . . . " Ryan seemed about to ask another question. He sighed and shook his head.

"But what?" Jason said.

"Well," he said hesitantly, "I've done some really bad and stupid things."

Jason patted Ryan's shoulder. "We all have," he said.

Duane nodded. "But Christ's death on the cross paid the price for all those bad and stupid things. When you confess them to him, and turn your back on them—he'll forgive you and transform you."

"That's it?" Ryan asked, lifting his head. "Just like that?"

Jason locked gazes with him. His expression was serious. "Yeah," he said.

Ryan nodded his head twice, slowly. "That's what I want," he said.

Jason nodded back, and said, "Let's pray, then."

❚❙◼❚❙◼❚❙◼❚❙◼

more than an inside story:
your story

SARAH AND ALISON have been Christians for much of their lives, but they've never experienced the full transformation that comes with the development of deep convictions about who Jesus is. Ryan is about to pray a sinner's prayer, only now coming to believe with conviction that God loves and accepts him unconditionally.

What's your story? Whether you need to *make a first-*

time commitment to a transformed life in Christ or *recommit* to a transformed life in Christ, here is what you can pray to God:

To Recommit to a Transformed Life in Christ

God, *I recognize* that I still have a problem with you. Even though I have prayed for your forgiveness in the past, I still find myself not putting you first in my life—I've wanted to go my own way.

I realize that you are my solution. You came to make dead people live in relationship with you and I want to live that way. Please forgive me for not keeping you first in my life and for being disobedient to you. I believe it is through you and you alone that I will find true happiness and meaning in life.

I respond to you right now with conviction—being thoroughly convinced that you are the true Christ, my resurrection and power source, who gives me everything I need to live a life pleasing to you.

I rely on you to transform me anew each day. Right now I yield to your Holy Spirit and I place you in control of my decision-making. I want Your way to be my way each and every day.

Thank you for loving me and making it possible for me to become a child of God. Please live your life in and through me every day. In the name of Jesus I pray, amen.

To Commit to a Transformed Life in Christ

God, *I recognize* that I have a problem with you. I have sinned against you and have gone my own way in life.

I realize now that you are my only solution. I ask you to forgive me of all my sins. Right now I am turning away from my old life and turning to Jesus Christ as my only hope of finding a relationship with God.

I respond to you, Jesus Christ, with conviction—I am convinced that you are the only way to God. Right now I place my trust in you as my Savior and believe you will transform me into a child of God and give me an eternal relationship with him and you. I believe it is through you and you alone that I will find true happiness and meaning.

I rely upon you to do the transforming work in my life. You said in John 11:25 that I will be given eternal life by believing in you and that I will never perish. I am believing and relying on you to transform me into your child right now.

Thank you for doing what you said you would do. Thank you for making me a forgiven child of God and bringing me into a relationship with the one true God. Please live the transformed life of Christ in and through me every day. I pray these things in Jesus' name, amen.

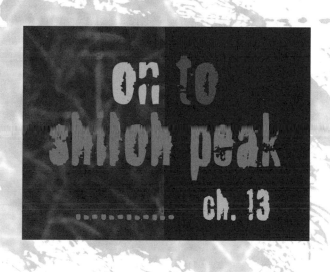

on to shiloh peak

ch. 13

RYAN AWOKE the next morning with an odd sensation. The air inside his tent seemed brighter and lighter. He stuck his head out through the tent flap and blinked; for a moment, he thought he might be dreaming. But he couldn't shake the feeling that everything seemed different. He stood and immediately felt as though he had grown a few inches, yet he seemed lighter, as though he were capable of walking on air.

When Jason saw his tentmate exit the tent, he leaped up and wrapped his arms around Ryan in a bearlike hug. "How ya doing?"

Ryan rubbed his eyes with his palms. "Weird," he answered. "I feel a little weird, but good."

"Hungry?" Jason asked.

Ryan nodded and followed Jason to the fire ring. They shared breakfast together, and Ryan enjoyed the attentions of everyone in the group as they patted him on the back, spoke words of encouragement, and asked him questions about his experience the night before.

Liz announced that Alison had something to share. Alison explained that she, like Sarah, had made a recommitment to a transformed life in Christ. Jason began singing and led the group in an exuberant song of praise.

Ryan didn't know all the words to the song, but he did his best to sing along. He was still getting used to the very idea of being a Christian, like Jason Withers and Duane Cunningham. But once the others settled into breakfast mode, Ryan sank into his own thoughts . . . and a new conflict in his heart.

ratsbane sat alone in the classroom and stared intently at the GreenFeed screen. He had been watching carefully since before Ryan had left his tent and appeared in the field of vision.

Furblight entered and loped quickly on all fours to Ratsbane's side, her sharp front badger claws clicking on the rocky floor under her feet. "What's happening?"

Ratsbane turned the screen slightly to afford Furblight a better view. "It's quiet so far. Last night another one recommitted to the Enemy. But only those three—" he said, pointing to Duane, Eli, and Liz—"have prayed so far this morning, so we have a window of opportunity."

"What about the new escapee?" she asked, referring to Ryan in the terminology used for humans who have recently escaped the darkness of sin and entered the "wonderful light" of relationship with God.[1]

"Take a look," Ratsbane said. He keyed in a text message on the Palm PET, and Furblight watched on the GreenFeed as the screen revealed Ryan sitting on a log next to Jason. At Ryan's side, visible only in the diaphanous green light of the video image, sat a demon in a chimpanzee body with a lizard head, absent-mindedly picking bug scraps out of his teeth with a fingernail. Suddenly the demon peered at his own handheld device and then lifted his head and grinned, waving at Ratsbane and Furblight like a fan appearing onscreen at a sporting event.

"Blotworm, there," Ratsbane explained, pointing to the demon on-screen, "has been with the escapee every second of the night. He's doing the best that can be expected under the circumstances."

"The circumstances?" Furblight echoed.

"New escapees present a grave challenge to our demonic efforts," Ratsbane explained. "Especially during the first few hours and days after the new birth has taken effect. They're like sponges, wanting to soak up every drop of friendship and relationship the Enemy offers."

Furblight's badger face twisted into a sour expression, as though she'd just tasted something disagreeable.

"But Blotworm's job is to slam the door shut on that sort of thing. And while he's working on-site," Ratsbane said, handing a Palm PET to Furblight, "you will be making sure to suggest all sorts of devious and destructive behavior to his mind and heart—not so he notices, of course."

"Subtle," Furblight said.

"And sly," Ratsbane said.

■ ▪ ● ▪ ■ ▪ ● ▪ ■ ▪ ● ▪ ■ ▪ ● ▪ ■

JASON grabbed his guitar and rose to face the Westcastle group, who were finishing their breakfast. "This has already been an amazing trip," he said, strumming a few chords. "But—if you can believe it—God's not finished with us yet."

He began singing a new song, one that Ryan hadn't heard before, so Ryan just listened to the others sing. Everyone else seemed to know the words and the tune.

You don't know the words, he found himself thinking. *You're the only one who doesn't know the words. You're still an outsider.*

He tried to hum along with the tune, but the melody was unpredictable.

Nothing's really changed.

He looked around the circle at the others. Alison and Liz sang with their eyes closed. Duane was watching Jason. Sarah met Ryan's gaze and smiled.

They're just like everyone else. They're accepting you only because you're just like them now.

Ryan shook his head, unconsciously. He wondered where that thought had come from. He'd never thought of that possibility. What if his new faith and new life were just another attempt to conform? What if he was just trying to conform to a new group? How did he know he wasn't just kidding himself . . . again?

You'll go back to Westcastle at the end of the week, and they'll drop you like an ugly prom date, just like everyone else.

Jason transitioned into another song, one that Ryan knew. But he still didn't join in. He was too busy arguing with himself . . . or with someone. He had experienced so much rejection and disapproval—especially from other kids—that he had long tried to convince himself not to hope for anything else.

But he did. He believed last night that he'd found what he'd been craving all his life. It started with his first-hand experience of God's love for him, and it was reinforced by the acceptance he experienced from the others: Duane, Liz, Jason, Alison, and Sarah. Eli, too.

But you know it'll never last. They'll accept you . . . until they find a reason not to.

But even then, Ryan told himself, God would still accept him. Like Jason said after they had prayed together last night, Jesus promised never to leave him or forsake him.

Yeah, right. They'd reject you right now if they had a reason.

Yeah, well, Ryan figured, there's one way to find out.

No.

Ryan stood abruptly. Jason had just finished singing, and Duane had just started the morning's devotional talk.

"Can I say something?" Ryan asked.

Duane looked surprised, and a voice inside Ryan said, No, don't do it. Sit down!

"Sure, Ryan," Duane said. "What's on your mind?"

Ryan made a few false starts and started to feel panic. He didn't know how to say what he wanted to say.

"Take your time, dude," Jason said.

That did it. Ryan looked at Jason; he was smiling. "Thanks," Ryan said. He inhaled deeply and tried again. "I don't understand everything that happened last night," he said. "But I think I understand enough. I think I know that, because God's new relationship with me has put the old life behind me, I don't have to feel guilty for my past sins. And I feel like that gives me a new confidence, sort of, something I've never had before. It makes me feel like I don't have to pretend anymore, because . . . I know I'm loved and accepted no matter what anyone else may think of me. And maybe now that Jesus is living in me and giving me the strength I never had, maybe I can tell you guys something . . . something I never planned to tell anyone."

Don't be stupid, said the voice inside his head. *You don't have to do this.*

"I know I don't have to do this," he said, the muscles

in his jaw tightening with determination. "But I think I can
. . . and, maybe more important, I think I should." He told
them about breaking into the video store. He told the
whole story of that night. He admitted why he did it. He
even explained that the possibility of avoiding discovery
was the main reason he even came on this trip.

"Anyway," he said finally, "I know there are going to
be consequences to all this. But I think I've got to stand up
and do what's right. I can't believe I'm saying all this, to be
honest with you, but I think when I get home I have to
admit what I did and see what happens. I just felt like I
should give you all the chance to know the truth about
me."

Ryan nodded solemnly and then sat down. For a long
moment, no one said anything. Every person seemed
frozen in place.

Then, suddenly, Jason slapped Ryan's back with the
flat of his hand. "Dude!" he said. "That's awesome!"

Ryan realized that Duane and Liz were standing in
front of him. "Ryan," Duane said, "I can't thank you
enough for trusting us enough to tell us all that. You've
paid us a real compliment by being honest with us, and I
want you to know we really appreciate it and respect you
for it."

"And," Liz added, "I want you to know that whatever happens, we'll be there to go through it with you.
We'll go to the police station with you, we'll go to court
with you if it comes to that, we'll do whatever we can to
help you follow through and do what's right every step of
the way. You won't have to do any of it alone."

"And God will be with you, too," Sarah said.

"You're right, Sarah," Duane said. "The Bible tells a
story about three guys who were thrown into a fiery
furnace because they stood up for what was right . . . but
they weren't in that furnace alone. The Bible says that the
Son of God was there in the furnace with them. And they

survived. And you will, too. You'll get through this, and the Lord will be with you through it all."

"So will we," said Alison.

"Yeah," the others agreed.

Ryan turned and looked at Sarah. She was smiling, and he smiled back. He thought for a moment that he saw admiration in her eyes, and he felt himself blushing. And suddenly he realized . . . the arguing in his head had stopped.

"i have something for you," Ratsbane said. He had watched with interest as the battle for Ryan had raged, Furblight working from a distance and Blotworm on location. When Ryan had stood to make his little speech, sparks had jumped and smoke had billowed from Furblight's Palm PET, and she had lost all contact with the boy. When that happened, Ratsbane had exited the cavernous classroom.

Now he had returned, and in his hand he held a bucket.

"What's that?" Furblight asked. The Palm PET still smoked, although the contest had been lost a good fifteen minutes ago. The video monitor in the corner and the GreenFeed on the desk depicted Duane and Liz standing in front of Ryan, pledging their support to him.

"A drudge bucket," Ratsbane answered.

"Drudge duty? Me?" she screamed. "But I . . ."

"You are the one who suggested, 'They'd reject you

right now if they had a reason.' It's on the tape. Would you like to hear it?"

"So what? I had him in the palm of my . . . paw."

"Yeah, until you yourself gave him the idea to put the Enemy's acceptance to the test." He pushed his bulbous face and glassy black eyes into her face. "Never encourage a subject to take the Enemy at his Word!"

"But wait," she pleaded. "Don't I get a second chance?"

"Second chance?" Ratsbane mocked. "Second chance? Fool! This is hell. You're all out of chances."

"But—"

"Good-bye!" he said, crossing his arms and peremptorily dismissing her.

Furblight stared at the ant-headed demon with an expression of betrayal on her face. She slumped to the classroom door and, without looking back, trudged out, bound for the putrid slag-and-sulfur pits that fueled the furnaces of the underworld.

Ratsbane fingered the fissure in his skull and thought. Things looked pretty dark for hell. But there was one last hope—Sarah. The underdemons began filing into the subterranean classroom, and Ratsbane quickly corralled them around the video monitor and the GreenFeed. He related the disastrous developments of that morning, the fatal mistake of Furblight, and the repulsive stand that Ryan Ortiz had taken even in the face of possible condemnation and prosecution.

"But we are never without resources. We can still keep this experiential relationship with the Enemy from spreading—*if* we focus on preventing that Sarah Milford girl from translating the relationship she's experienced into a mode of operating, a way of life. You see, she's had a moving experience, but if we can confine it to just that— a one-time experience—we can keep it from spreading and thus stem the tide and prevent further damage.

"So," he announced, "I want every Palm PET focused on the Milford girl. Hit her with all you've got. And whatever you do, don't tempt her to take the Enemy at his Word."

∎▪◦∎▪◦∎▪◦∎▪◦∎

AFTER THE WESTCASTLE GROUP finished devotions, Eli said his good-byes and told Sarah that he would see her next week for his planned meeting at her home. He also refused Duane's repeated efforts to accompany him to the aid station for medical attention; he assured Duane that his wounds were not as bad as they looked and insisted on journeying alone.

Once Eli left, the team broke camp and continued the last few miles of their hike toward Shiloh Peak with renewed vigor and determination. But Sarah Milford felt her mood dipping lower and lower as the hike progressed. After several unsuccessful attempts, Alison stopped trying to engage Sarah in conversation. And when they stopped for lunch, the meal that would potentially be their last before reaching the summit, Sarah sat alone on a tiny outcropping overlooking the winding trail they had just climbed.

As they resumed the hike after lunch, Sarah fell into step with Liz. They walked in silence for some time. Liz sensed that Sarah wanted to talk but seemed satisfied to let her choose the timing.

"Do you think we'll see the other team when we reach the top?" Sarah asked.

Liz took her time responding. "I don't know," she said. "Why?"

Another period of silence followed. "I'm not sure what to say to Jennifer and Jessica when I see them," Sarah said.

"Is it because of how they treat you," Liz asked, "or

because of how you've treated them?"

"Both," Sarah said, grabbing a sapling by the side of the path and pulling herself up a steep part of the trail. "I just don't know what I'm supposed to do."

"How about asking for her forgiveness?"

"Ask her to forgive *me?*" Sarah responded a little surprised. "Should I? I mean, could I even do that?"

"I don't know," Liz answered. "*You* probably couldn't but . . . " She didn't finish. They hiked on in silence for a few moments. Sarah was the next to speak.

"She won't ever ask for *my* forgiveness, will she?"

"Does it really matter?" Liz responded.

"What do you mean?" Sarah asked.

"I mean, whether she ever asked you to forgive her or not, shouldn't you forgive her anyway? Like Eli forgave *you* before you ever asked *him?*"

"Like God forgives us," Sarah said softly, more to herself than to Liz. She turned her gaze to the trail in front of her again, not knowing what would happen at the summit, but determined to rely on God for whatever came next.

the victory flag

ch. 14

JASON SPOTTED the flag first. He called to Ryan, "There it is! It's still there!"

"We're going to win," Ryan said.

He called behind him on the trail. He knew the others weren't far behind, but the rules stated that the victory flag could be removed from its sheath only when all team members gripped it. His calls still echoed down the trail when he saw Mr. Robinson leading his team up the hillside, at the point where two trails converged just below the summit.

Ryan froze. Mr. Robinson approached and lifted his gaze to Ryan's face. They locked gazes for a moment. Then Mr. Robinson smiled.

"Ryan," he said with a nod.

Mr. Robinson passed Ryan on the trail, and then two others from his group followed closely. Ryan looked up the trail toward Jason, who stood in the clearing near the flag, looking helpless. Half of the other team's group had already arrived, and Ryan and Jason were still waiting for the others. He expected Alison and Sarah to appear any second with Duane and Liz close behind . . . but they hadn't answered his calls, and a fourth member of the other group appeared on the trail and headed for the victory flag.

●▪▪●▪▪●▪▪●▪▪●

SARAH, hiking the last part of the journey with Alison, caught a glimpse of the flag through the trees ahead. "We're almost there," she said.

The two girls picked up their pace and arrived at the junction of the trails at the same moment that Jennifer and Jessica appeared from the opposite direction. The four of them saw each other in the same instant.

Jessica turned to Jennifer. "Run," she said. She took off for the summit.

Jennifer paused to grin at Sarah and Alison. "Twice in the same week," she said, recalling her snide comment at the beginning of the adventure. "To the same girl." She turned to follow Jessica.

Sarah had just opened her mouth to respond to Jennifer's remark when she saw her rival slip on an exposed root on the path and pitch forward with a pained cry. She rolled quickly over and grabbed her ankle.

"Are you all right?" Alison asked, reaching out to help her.

Jennifer recoiled from Alison's offered hand. "I don't need your help," she said.

"Are you sure?" Alison asked, her tone still sweet, apparently unaffected by Jennifer's rudeness.

"Let's go, Alison," Sarah said.

"But—"

"Leave her alone," Sarah insisted. "She doesn't want our help."

Alison joined Sarah, and they started for the summit.

After a few steps, Sarah glanced back in Jennifer's direction and saw her stand to her feet and try to walk. She collapsed again in a heap, holding her ankle with both hands.

"Wait," Sarah said. Alison stopped. A battle ensued inside Sarah. She wanted to leave Jennifer behind. She wanted to walk away. She wanted to treat her the way she deserved to be treated. But then she remembered Liz's words to her: *Shouldn't you forgive her?*

Sarah hesitated a moment and then walked back toward Jennifer. "Is it broken?" she asked.

Jennifer was visibly reluctant to answer, but she shook her head. "No, I don't think so," she said. "I think I just twisted it."

Sarah glanced, unsmiling, at Alison and sighed wearily. "Get on the other side," she told her friend.

Alison obeyed, and she and Sarah draped Jennifer's arms around their necks and helped her to her feet.

"Put your weight on our shoulders," Sarah said, "and just use your good foot. Stay off the other one."

"Okay," Jennifer answered.

"Let's go," Sarah said. "Not too fast."

⬛▪◼▪◻◼▪◻◼▪◻◼▪◻

RYAN couldn't believe his eyes. The final scene of their SWAT trip seemed to be unfolding in slow motion. He watched as Sarah and Alison appeared in the clearing, supporting Jennifer Brown between them—all three of them in full packs. Jennifer hopped on one foot every time Sarah and Alison took a step, and in this way they proceeded, stride by stride, toward the flag.

When the other team saw the odd procession, they rushed to Jennifer's side and took over for Alison and Sarah about a dozen or so steps from the flag. Then, with Jessica on one side and Mr. Robinson on the other, Jennifer hobbled to the flag.

Sarah watched numbly as the other team gripped the flag, counted to three, and lifted it from its sheath.

❦

THE OTHER TEAM was loudly celebrating their victory when Ryan turned his gaze away . . . and saw that Duane and Liz had arrived at the summit.

"What took you guys so long?" he asked. "We could have won!"

Duane slapped him on the back. "I'm sorry, man," he said. "We got here just in time to see Alison and Sarah helping Jennifer."

Liz had tears in her eyes.

"But we could have won!" Ryan repeated.

"We did," Duane said. "We absolutely did."

❦

THE CAMPSITE at Shiloh Peak was one of the largest in the entire Shiloh Wilderness. A large grove of pines and cedars sheltered campers from the biting winds that routinely battered hikers at this elevation, and a narrow but rapid stream nearby offered clean, cold water.

The two teams set up separate camps for the night, but the Westcastle Community Church team campsite was close enough for the other team's jubilation and celebration at winning the SWAT competition to reach their ears.

"That was an amazing thing you did," Liz told Sarah, while they waited for Ryan and Jason to cook their evening meal. They sat together on a log at the campsite's outer edge.

Sarah looked up and slowly nodded. "It's amazing to me, too. But I do wish we could have won."

"Well," Liz said. "I agree with Duane. I think we were the winners in all this."

"You did the right thing, Sarah," Liz continued. "You duplicated the same thing we've been talking about all week. You not only experienced a loving, forgiving relationship with God, but you also showed that kind of relationship to someone else. You did the same sort of thing for Jennifer that both God and Eli did for you. You gave her a tremendous gift, and that's because of the transformation that has taken place in your life."

"Yeah, well," Sarah said, "I really do sense a difference inside. It's a new feeling for me, not hating Jennifer anymore. I like it, but I don't know what to do with it. I don't know where to go from here unless it's to ask Jennifer to forgive me for what I've done and how I've felt toward her."

Liz smiled warmly, and Sarah sensed both happiness and pride in her expression. "I think you have your answer," Liz said.

They headed for the campsite for dinner. Sarah was quieter than usual.

God, she prayed from deep within herself. *How am I going to do this? What am I going to say? I don't even know where to begin.* She drifted in and out of the dinner conversation around the fire. Jason and Ryan had devised a surprisingly tasty concoction they called "Soyburger Helper," and their comical depictions of the ingredients and preparation of the meal had everyone laughing— everyone except Sarah.

After dinner, Sarah wandered off by herself. She inched slowly along the semidarkened trail to the rear of the campsite, lost in thought, until a sound behind her jolted her back to reality.

"Sarah?" It was Ryan.

"Hi," she said.

"I can't believe what you did today," he said.

"I know," she answered. She felt like too much was going on, and she didn't know how to keep her thoughts and emotions straight. "I'm really sorry if I let you down. I just—"

"No," he said, "I think it was great."

"You do?"

"Yeah," he said. "At first I thought you and Alison were crazy, but then I realized how cool it was."

"That I helped the other team win?"

"No, that you—in spite of everything Jennifer has done to you—you treated her like a friend instead of an enemy. You're amazing."

She looked at him, and they stared into each other's eyes. "You're . . . you're pretty amazing, too," she said.

A long silent moment passed between them. Ryan's face seemed to change before her eyes, and she realized she was seeing him in a new way. And she liked what she saw.

⬛▪◼▪◼▪▪◼▪◼▪◼▪◼

LATER THAT EVENING Sarah headed toward Jennifer's campsite. She had traversed—alone—the seemingly interminable distance between the two camps, though it couldn't have been more than a couple of dozen yards. She had approached Jennifer Brown from behind and tapped her on the shoulder. "Can I talk to you for a minute?" Sarah asked. Jessica, who sat beside her best friend, had seen Sarah appear out of the darkness only a second before Sarah spoke to Jennifer.

"What do *you* want?" Jennifer asked.

"Actually, I want to talk to both of you," Sarah said. She was nervous, but she felt a deep peace in her heart. "I want to ask you both to forgive me."

Jennifer eyed her suspiciously. "For what?"

"I snuck into your camp last night," she explained, "and put something in your water bottles. It's a kind of an herb called elderberry, and it—"

"You—" Jennifer started to stand, but grimaced with pain and sat back down.

Jessica turned to her friend. "Is she saying what I

think she's saying?" she asked. "Is that why we've been . . . going . . . all day?"

This wasn't going well. Sarah nodded. "Yeah," she admitted. "It's my fault. I was trying to get even, and—"

"*That's* why you helped me," Jennifer said, her tone accusing. "You wanted to ease your conscience?"

"Actually, no. I'm here to ask your forgiveness because it was wrong of me to do what I did to you. And I helped you when you hurt yourself because . . . well, because somebody did that for me."

"What are you talking about, Milford?" Jennifer asked.

"I'm not sure I can explain it," she answered. "And I'd understand if you didn't want to forgive me. But I helped you today because—" *This is going to sound stupid,* she warned herself. But she continued anyway. "Because there's someone in my life who loves and accepts me for who I am and forgives me for what I've done, even though I've treated him awful." She shrugged. "You're going to think I'm crazy, but it's true. I've just recommitted my life to Christ and I can admit that I was wrong to try to get even with you. So I'd like to ask you to forgive me."

Jennifer's eyes narrowed into tiny slits as she scrutinized Sarah's face. She seemed to be waiting for the punch line. Finally, she seemed to give up. "You're crazy, Milford," she said.

Jennifer's tone wasn't unkind, but Sarah felt herself blush anyway. She decided she would wait a little longer and not press Jennifer again.

Jennifer looked at Jessica. Then she seemed to glance at her feet, before looking up again. She flipped her hair back over her shoulders in a typical gesture, and then grinned self-consciously. "But you're okay," she said.

Sarah smiled and nodded. She understood. "Thanks," she said. She hesitated only a moment longer and then turned to walk back to camp.

ratsbane stared at the video screen, slowly shaking his gigantic ant head from side to side. "I don't understand," he said. "I don't understand."

He turned to the demon Rankmeat, who had taken Furblight's seat on the front row. "Let me see that," he said, snatching the Palm PET device from the grasp of his cloven hoof. He turned the device over and popped it open.

"No batteries!" Ratsbane screamed in frustration. He rapped Rankmeat's turkey head with the useless device. "What happened to your batteries?"

"I–I don't know," Rankmeat gobbled. "They were there before."

Ratsbane leapfrogged Rankmeat and landed beside Stench, grabbing his Palm PET and opening it. "Empty!" he croaked.

He hopped from one demon to another and discovered that not one of the handheld devices held batteries.

"What about yours?" Stench asked.

Ratsbane glared at his Palm PET, which he had left on the desk at the front of the classroom. He quickly vaulted to the front and opened his device. Two batteries popped out.

"So," Rankmeat clucked, "this disaster is all your fault."

"What?" Ratsbane said.

"We can't be blamed for equipment failure," Rankmeat said. "But you—you had a working device. Which means you're the only one in this room who could possibly be responsible for that mess on the mountain."

"Don't be ridiculous," Ratsbane said. "I am a Senior Fellow at Brimstone U. I am the Master here! You've all read about me in *Hunchcrump's History of Hell!* This is just a momentary setback."

He turned and looked at the scene between Jennifer, Jessica, and Sarah. It was obvious that things were not going hell's way. He cleared his froggy throat and chuckled, affecting a bravado he did not feel. "It's actually a good thing," he said. "We've got these hateful Westcastle kids right . . . where . . . we . . ."

He turned to face his demon students. They wore hungry looks, and those with fangs bared them. The entire classroom approached him like ravenous wolves.

"Now," he protested, "wait. There's no need to get hasty. Look." He showed them his wart-covered skin. "This stuff is like rubber. It's like eating an old tennis shoe."

Stench pushed in front of the others and extended a drudge bucket to Ratsbane. "Stinks to be you," he said.

Ratsbane's shoulders slumped as he took the bucket from his former student. He'd been through demotions like this before. It was one of the things that made hell what it was.

❙▪●❙▪●❙▪●❙▪●

MILES AWAY in the gloomy corridors of hell, Furblight trudged toward one of the innumerable slag-and-sulfur pits of the netherworld. It was indescribably hard to walk, with the front feet of a badger and the hind feet of a duck. But though she was never happy, she wore a hellish grin as she thought of Ratsbane's plight. *I tried to tell them his old strategies and new technology wouldn't work,* she said to herself, as she dumped several dozen perfectly good Palm PET batteries into the sulfur pits.

doing the
right thing

ch. 15

SARAH HAD TAKEN only a few steps away from Jennifer and Jessica when she saw Ryan. He waited for her at the edge of the other team's campsite.

"What are you doing here?" she asked.

He shrugged. "I wanted to be here, in case you needed some help."

"You knew what I was going to do?"

He shook his head. "No, but when I saw you walking this direction, I wanted to make sure you were okay."

She smiled with appreciation . . . and affection. "Thanks," she said. "I am okay."

"I think so, too," he said. She started to walk back to their own campsite, but he didn't follow.

"Don't you want to go back?" she asked.

"No," he said. "Listening to you talk to Jennifer made me realize I need to do the same thing."

"Oh," she said, approvingly.

"I thought I'd have a talk with Mr. Robinson,"

Ryan said.

"Mr. Robinson?"

"He's a policeman," he responded.

"Ohhhh," she said. "That's going to be hard, isn't it?"

He shrugged. "Yeah," he said. "I was hoping you'd go with me."

"Really?"

He nodded.

She threw her arms around him. They hugged. "I'd love to," she said softly.

Notes

Chapter 1: TROUBLE IN WESTCASTLE

1. Barna Research Group, "Life Goals of American Teens," study commissioned by Josh McDowell Ministry (Ventura, Calif.: The Barna Research Group, Ltd., 2001), 6.
2. Ibid., 8.
3. Ibid.
4. Glen Schultz, *Kingdom Education* (Nashville: LifeWay, 1998), 39.
5. Ibid., 40.
6. Josh McDowell and Bob Hostetler, *Right from Wrong* (Nashville: W, 1994), 271.
7. "The Churched Youth Study," (Dallas: Josh McDowell Ministry, 1994), 69.
8. Ibid., 65.

Chapter 2: THE SWAT TEAM

1. Barna Research Group, "Third Millennium Teens" (Ventura, Calif.: The Barna Research Group, Ltd., 1999), 51.
2. Josh D. McDowell and Bob Hostetler, Right from Wrong (Nashville: W, 1994), 263.
3. Barna, "Third Millennium Teens," 48.
4. Ibid., 44.
5. Ibid.

Chapter 3: THE SEARCH FROM WITHIN

1. Barna, "Third Millennium Teens," 49.

Chapter 13: ON TO SHILOH PEAK

1. See 1 Peter 2:9.

About the Authors

JOSH MCDOWELL never intended to be a defender of the Christian faith. In fact, his goal was just the opposite. As a skeptic at Kellogg College in Michigan, he was challenged by a group of Christian students to intellectually examine the claims of Christianity. He accepted the challenge and set out to prove that Christ's claims to be God and the historical reliability of Scripture could be neither trusted nor accurately verified. The evidence he discovered changed the course of his life. He discovered that the Bible was the most historically reliable document of all antiquity and that Christ's claim that he was God could be objectively verified. When Josh was brought face-to-face with the objective and relevant truth of Christ and his Word, he trusted in Christ as the Son of God and his personal Savior.

Josh transferred to Wheaton College and completed a bachelor's degree in language. He went on to receive a master's degree in theology from Talbot Theological Seminary in California. In 1964 he joined the staff of Campus Crusade for Christ (CCC) and eventually became an international traveling representative for CCC, focusing primarily on issues facing today's young people.

Josh has spoken to more than seven million young people in eighty-four countries, including more than seven hundred university and college campuses. He has authored or coauthored more than sixty books and workbooks with more than thirty million in print worldwide. Josh's most popular works are *The New Evidence That Demands a Verdict*, *More Than a Carpenter*, *Why True Love Waits*, the *Right from Wrong* book, the *Right from Wrong* workbook series, and *Beyond Belief to Convictions*.

Josh has been married to Dottie for more than thirty years and has four children. Josh and Dottie live in Dallas, Texas.

BOB HOSTETLER is a writer, editor, pastor, and speaker. His writing includes the award-winning *Don't Check Your Brains at the Door*, *The New Tolerance* (coauthored with Josh McDowell), *Beyond Belief to Convictions* (coauthored with Josh McDowell), and other books with Josh. Bob has won two Gold Medallion Awards, three Ohio Associated Press awards, and an Amy Foundation Award.

Bob is a frequent speaker at churches, conferences, and retreats. He has been a disc jockey, pastor, magazine editor, freelance book editor, and (with his wife, Robin) a foster parent to ten boys (though not all at once). He and his wife are among the leaders of Cobblestone Community Church in Oxford, Ohio.

Bob and Robin have two children, Aubrey and Aaron, who are currently attending Miami University in Oxford, Ohio.

DAVE BELLIS is a ministry consultant focusing on ministry planning and product development. He has pioneered an interactive video and workbook educational design used by more than one hundred thousand churches and small groups worldwide. For over twenty-five years as a campaign coordinator, writer, and producer, Dave Bellis has directed Josh McDowell's many campaigns, developing more than one hundred products including coauthoring *Beyond Belief to Convictions* with Bob and Josh. He and his wife, Becky, have two grown children and live in "the house that Meech built" in Copley, Ohio.

Begin a "Christianity 101" Process

The three integrated courses described below and on the
following pages will help you reveal the heart of God
and lead your people through a spiritual formation process.

REVEALING THE **GOD OF REDEMPTION**
WHO GAVE HIS LIFE TO REDEEM US

FOR CHILDREN	FOR YOUTH	FOR ADULTS
Is Christ Really God?	**Is Christ Really God?**	**Is Christ Really Go**
The Real Truth about Why Jesus Came	A Personal Encounter with the Transforming Christ	How to Lead your Youth to a Personal Encounter with the Transforming Ch

Uncovering the deep meaning of God's redemptive heart will open our hearts and minds
to who God truly is and prompt us to commit our lives to him.
Receiving the God of Redemption leads us to live a life of:
- Faith in God
- Worship of God
- Prayer to God

REVEALING THE **GOD OF RELATIONSHIPS**
WHO GAVE HIS SPIRIT & THE WORD TO BECOME INTIMATE WITH US

FOR CHILDREN	FOR YOUTH	FOR ADULTS
Is the Bible Personally from God?	**Christ Up Close & Personal**	**Christ Up Close & Personal**
The Real Truth about Living Like Jesus	The Real Truth about God's Spirit and His Word	How to Lead your Youth Discover the Real Truth ab God's Spirit and His Wor

God gave us his Spirit and his Word to empower us to become more and more like Christ.
Embracing the God of Relationships leads us to live a life of:
- Loving Others as Christ Loves Us
- Making Godly Choices

REVEALING THE **GOD OF RESTORATION**
WHO CONQUERED DEATH & GAVE US HIS CHURCH TO RECLAIM HIS KINGDOM

FOR CHILDREN	FOR YOUTH	FOR ADULTS
Will There Really Be a Perfect World?	**Christ Will Make All Things Right**	**Christ Will Make All Things Right**
The Real Truth about a Recreated Heaven & Earth	Your Mission and True Sense of Belonging in Life	How to Lead your Youth to Embrace Their Missio & True Sense of Belongin

God is on a mission and has given to us (his church) the same mission of reclaiming lost souls
and bringing them into the family of God. (*This course is in development and will be released in 2008.
Not pictured on the following pages*).
Accepting the Mission of the God of Restoration leads us to live a life of:
- Spiritual Warfare
- Spiritual Reproduction

True Foundations

Living Truth for Lifelong Growth

Revealing the **God of Redemption**
Who Gave His Life to Redeem Us

13-SESSION *ADULT* GROUP COURSE

Is Christ Really God?

This 5-part DVD series and 8-session Interactive Group Course equips adults with solid answers for who Christ really is and how to lead young people into a transformed relationship with God. The DVD series features Josh McDowell in each session and comes with a comprehensive Leaders Guide. The 8-session Interactive Group Course has a self-contained Leaders Guide with reproducible hand-outs for group participants. (This is a revised course previously titled *Belief Matters*.)   (Available Nov. 2006)

13-SESSION *YOUTH* GROUP COURSE

Is Christ Really God?

This youth edition 5-part DVD series combines a powerful message, compelling media illustrations, and captivating group activities to convince your students that only Christ as the true Son of God can transform our "dead lives" into a meaningful life in relationship with him. The 8-session Interactive Group Course guides them in how to live out their devotion to God, leading them to a face-to-face encounter with Christ and helping them experience a committed relationship with him. (This is a revised course previously titled *The Revolt*.)   (Available Nov. 2006)

8-SESSION *CHILDREN'S* GROUP COURSE

Is Christ Really God?

These workbooks for children grades 1-3 and 4-6 present foundational truth of Christ's deity and why he came to earth. Written in simple terms, they enable you to lead your children into a transformed relationship with Christ. The comprehensive Leaders Guide is for both the younger and older children's workbooks. Each child is to receive a workbook. (This is a revised course previously titled *True or False*.)   (Available Nov. 2006)

Living a life of faith, worship and prayer to God.
Start today at www.truefoundations.com

True Foundations
Living Truth for Lifelong Growth

Revealing the **God of Relationships**
Who Gave His Spirit and the Word
to Become Intimate with Us

13-SESSION *ADULT* GROUP COURSE

Christ Up Close & Personal.
This 5-part DVD series and 8-session Interactive Group Course equips adults with a clear understanding of the purpose of the Holy Spirit and his Word. Sessions featuring Josh McDowell, with accompanying Leaders Guide containing reproducible handouts, leads your group to discover the key to instilling Christlike living in their young people.   (Available Aug. 2006)

13-SESSION *YOUTH* GROUP COURSE

Christ Up Close & Personal.
With dynamic media illustrations and group activities, this youth edition 5-part DVD series drives home a compelling message: it is impossible to live the Christian life without the presence of the Holy Spirit and knowledge of God's Word. The 8-session Interactive Group Course leads students to love others and make right choices in the power of God's Spirit.

(Available Aug. 2006)

8-SESSION *CHILDREN'S* GROUP COURSE

Is the Bible Personally from God?
These workbooks for children grades 1-3 and 4-6 deliver a powerful message on how God's Spirit enables them to live by his Word in relationship with others. Children will learn how to yield to the Holy Spirit and how that makes both God and them very happy.

(Available Aug. 2006)

Living a life of making godly choices and loving others in Christlikeness.
Start today at www.truefoundations.com.

Other Ministries that Can Help You

INTIMATE LIFE MINISTRIES

David Ferguson and the Intimate Life Ministries (ILM) team of Austin, Texas can serve you through training and resources. They are primarily focused on providing a support network for ministers (pastors and youth workers), ministries, and Christian leaders.

ILM has developed very effective intergenerational resources, training, and seminar/training events for ministers, such as the "Galatians 6:6" and "Servant Church" retreats. To learn more visit **www.GreatCommandment.net**. For ILM's Center for Relational Care go to **www.relat care.org** or call 1-800-881-1808.

SONLIFE MINISTRIES

A youth worker training and church growth service focusing on fulfilling the Great Commission Visit **www.sonlife.com**.

NATIONAL NETWORK OF YOUTH MINISTRIES

An excellent ministry to get you connected with other youth ministers in your area and gain from their experience. Visit **www.youthworkers.net**.

JESUS FOCUSED YOUTH MINISTRY

A training and resource ministry to youth workers. Visit **www.reach-out.org**.

DARE 2 SHARE MINISTRIES

A training ministry to equip Christian teens to share their faith with courage, clarity and compassion. Visit **www.dare2share.org**.

Our goal is to help you reach yours.
Visit www.truefoundations.com.